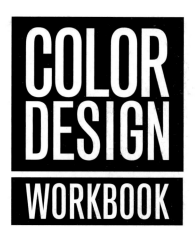

COLOR DESIGN
WORKBOOK

ROCKPORT

The color swatches contained in this book are as accurate as
possible. However, due to the nature of the four-color printing
proccess, slight variations can occur due to ink balancing on press.
Every effort has been made to minimize these variations.

"In order to use color effectively it
is necessary to recognize that color
deceives continually." —Josef Albers

© 2006 by Rockport Publishers, Inc.
First paperback edition published 2008

First published in the United States of America by
Rockport Publishers, a member of
Quayside Publishing Group
100 Cummings Center
Suite 406-L
Beverly , Massachusetts 01915-6101
Telephone: (978) 282-9590
Fax: (978) 283-2742
www.rockpub.com

Library of Congress Cataloging-in-Publication Data
Stone, Terry Lee.
    Color design workbook : a real-world guide to using color
in graphic design / by Terry Lee Stone, with Sean Adams
and Noreen Morioka ; designed by Sean Adams ;
acquisitions coordination by Victoria Lam.
        p.   cm.
    ISBN 1-59253-192-X (hardcover)
    1.Graphic Arts—Technique. 2. Commercial art—Themes,
motives. 3. Color in advertising. 4. Color in design.
5. Color—Psychological aspects. I. Adams, Sean.
II. Morioka, Noreen. III. Title.
NC1000.S76 2006
741.6—dc22   2005014277

ISBN-13: 978-1-59253-433-3
ISBN-10: 1-59253-433-3

10 9 8 7 6 5 4 3 2

COLOR DESIGN WORKBOOK

A Real-World Guide to Using Color in Graphic Design

By Terry Lee Stone
with Sean Adams and Noreen Morioka

BEVERLY MASSACHUSETTS

ROCKPORT PUBLISHERS

Color
Design
Workbook

Contents

Introduction

We follow this idea: it's okay to like what you like. This concept of accepting, regardless of motive, our innate desires and aesthetic preference is most apparent with color. Color is the subject that causes trouble. A shade of green can cause a client to run from the room, while others want the same tone on everything. It is subjective and volatile. Our choices, as designers, are to "lay low" and choose non-offensive colors or to design with aggressive vibrancy. Color provides strong visual statements that communicate our clients' messages.

Each color we use conveys both tone and meaning; which is essential to affecting audiences' judgments and reactions. Color is more than just a visual phenomenon—it is a uniquely emotional language and a symbolic tool for all designers. It is not simply a decorative afterthought and should be leveraged to its fullest extent.

A strong color palette in a visual system is one of a designer's most emotionally resonant tools. The right color creates the right response. In the global marketplace, we understand color in a cultural context as well. What works in Japan may possess a negative association in Saudi Arabia. Unlike designers of fifty years ago, we now face technological challenges with the breadth of usage opportunities across media—print, environmental, and digital; that shade of red looked so good on the screen, what happened on the printed poster?

There is more to color than a swatch in a book, or a pull down menu choice. Color is the element closest to the client and audience's subjective identity. Like a volatile radioactive element, it is extremely powerful and should be handled very, very carefully. **—Sean Adams**

In a physical sense, there really is no such thing as color, just light waves of different wavelengths.

The human eye can distinguish among these wavelengths, so we see the world in color. Rays of light vibrate at different speeds. The sensation of color, which happens in our brains, is a result of our vision's response to these different wavelengths. When taken together, the various rays our eyes can distinguish are called the *visible spectrum*. This fairly narrow range of colors includes red, orange, yellow, green, blue, blue-violet (which scientists call indigo), and violet.

The visible spectrum. The colors that the human eye can experience are expressed in this gradient graphic. Reds have the longest wavelengths, violets the shortest. Contained in a ray of light but invisible to the human eye are infrareds (below red in the visible spectrum) and ultraviolets (above violet in the visible spectrum). In addition in the visible spectrum, the eye perceives black and white. White contains all colors of the spectrum and is sometimes described as an achromatic color. Black is the absence of all color—no visible light reaches the eye. Alternatively, an exhaustive combination of multiple pigments can reflect so little light that the eye perceives black.

Apparent Colors

Color is derived from light, either natural or artificial. With little light, little or no color is present. With a lot of light comes lots of color. Strong light produces intense color.

Seeing in Color

Our eyes have three types of color receptor cells, or cones: red, green, and blue. As a result, all incoming light is reduced to these three colors. All perceived colors are generated by a mixture of these three colors. However, not every color can be seen by humans; those that can are therefore called the *visible spectrum*. People can distinguish approximately 10 million colors; this visible spectrum is called the *human color space*. Not everyone's color-sensing cells respond alike, so identification of a specific color is highly subjective.

The study of color is where art and science meet, with numerous theories from both disciplines coming into play. It can thus be difficult to comprehend. To understand color perception, we need to understand the physics of light, which causes and affects our ideas of primary colors.

Primary Colors

There are two types of primary color: additive and subtractive. As noted, our eyes have red, green, and blue (RGB) color receptors. RGB are the primary colors of pure light and are referred to as *additive* primary colors. The *subtractive* primary colors, made from reflected light, fall into two types: the printer's primaries, which are cyan, magenta, and yellow (CMY), and the artist's primaries, which are red, yellow, and blue (RYB). Artists' primaries, though nonscientific, are used as the basis for most color theory (*see chapter two*).

Designers utilize all three types of primary colors. They select colors using RYB and color theories. Then they generate layouts on computer screens in RGB, and then perhaps translate them into ink on paper with CMY—plus K, or black—to form the CMYK of four-color process lithography.

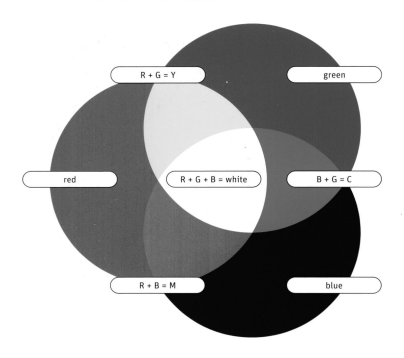

Additive Mixing (RGB Model)

R + G = Y

green

red

R + G + B = white

B + G = C

R + B = M

blue

▲ **Additive Color: The RGB Primaries (Light)**
Visible spectrum colors are pure and represent the greatest possible brightness or intensity. Designers working with rays of colored light, as on computer screens, use additive colors, or RGB. When these colors overlap, other colors are produced: red and blue light form cyan; red and green light form yellow; and green and blue light form magenta. When all three additive primaries overlap, white light is produced. Thus, white light is the combined presence of all color wavelengths. We call them additive because all together, these primaries create white. RGB reflects actual human color receptors. Mixtures of these primary colors produce a large part of the human color experience. Television sets, computer monitors, cameras, and color scanners all produce mixtures of red, green, and blue light.

> **"He who wants to become master of color must see, feel, and experience each individual color in its many endless combinations with all other colors."**—Johannes Itten

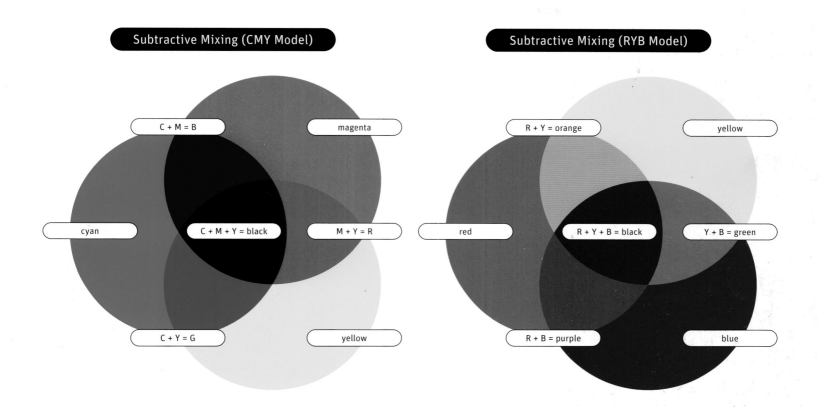

Subtractive Mixing (CMY Model)

- C + M = B
- magenta
- cyan
- C + M + Y = black
- M + Y = R
- C + Y = G
- yellow

Subtractive Mixing (RYB Model)

- R + Y = orange
- yellow
- red
- R + Y + B = black
- Y + B = green
- R + B = purple
- blue

▲ **Subtractive Color: The CMY Primaries (Transparent Pigments)**

All objects have physical properties that cause them to absorb some color waves and reflect others. Color, when applied to a surface such as canvas or paper, has the same characteristic. The sensation of color is produced when a surface absorbs all the wavelengths except those the eyes perceive. When color is experienced through reflected light, it is called *subtractive*. There are two sets of subtractive primary colors: the artist's primaries—red, yellow, and blue (RYB)—and the printer's primaries—cyan, magenta, and yellow (CMY) transparent inks and dyes. Coupled with black, known as K, we get CMYK, or four-color process. Each of these triads is combined to produce all visible color. In the subtractive CMY model, magenta combines with yellow form red, yellow and cyan form green, and cyan and magenta form violet (purple). In the case of both versions of the subtractive primaries, when all the primary colors are combined, black is produced—that is, no color is reflected.

▲ **Subtractive Color: The RYB Primaries (Opaque Pigments)**

In the RYB triad, red combines with yellow to produce orange, red and blue create violet (purple), and blue and yellow create green. RYB, the primary color system used in art classes, forms the basis of most color theory. As with CMY, when all the primary colors are combined, black is produced—no color is reflected. The secondary colors produced by the three triads indicate the purity of the colors that can be obtained by the different mixing methods. RGB produces pure CMY as secondary colors, and the CMY triad produces RGB as secondary colors, but they are duller than pure RGB light. The secondary colors resulting from RYB are even duller than those in the RGB or CMY triads.

The Properties of Color

Whether using the additive or subtractive primaries, each color must be described in terms of its physical properties. These properties are independent of each other, and each one must be measured or defined in order to fully describe the color. Scientific descriptions of color, or *colorimetry*, involve the specification of these color properties in either a subjective or objective system of measurement. The subjective system describes color in terms of hue, saturation, and brightness (HSB), while the objective system measures the dominant wavelength, purity, and luminance of colors.

Hue is the common name of a color that indicates its position in the visible spectrum or on the color wheel. Hue is determined by the specific wavelength of the color in a ray of light. The description of a hue can be made more precise in comparison to the next hue (e.g., a certain blue might be more accurately called blue-green). *Saturation* refers to the intensity, strength, purity, or chroma—the absence of black, white, or gray—in a color. A vivid color has high or full saturation, whereas a dull one is desaturated. Saturation is a measure of the richness of a color. *Brightness,* or value, is the relative degree of light-ness or darkness of a color, or its reflective quality or brilliance. A color can be more narrowly described as either light or dark (e.g., light blue or dark blue). The brightness of a color is changed by mixing it with white (to form a *tint*) or with black (to form a *shade*) in varying proportions. Graphic design software programs have tools for varying the HSB of colors.

Objective color notation was developed by the Com-mission Internationale de l'Eclairage (CIE) to provide a mathematical model for describing color. The CIE (in English, the International Commission on Illumination) is an international technical, scien-tific, and cultural nonprofit organization that sets standards on the science and art of lighting, vision, and colorimetry. Though CIE notation is not used by designers, it underpins color management in modern digital devices.

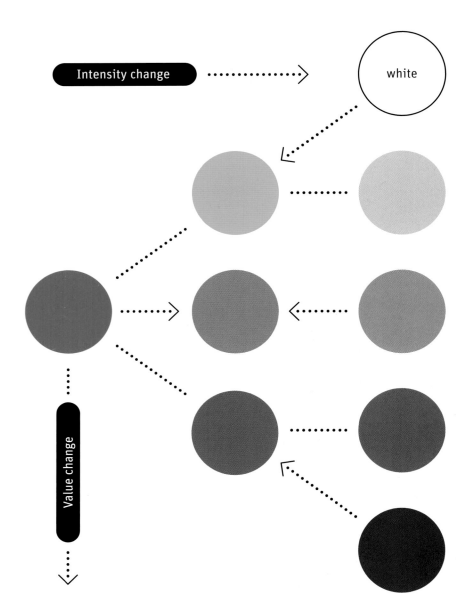

▲ This chart demonstrates changes in satura-tion and value by adding or subtracting black, white, or gray. When white is added to a bright red, the value is lighter, and the resulting color is less saturated. Adding black to the red results in a dark red closer to the neutral scale because of saturation changes. If gray is added, the saturation is lowered, but the value is unchanged.

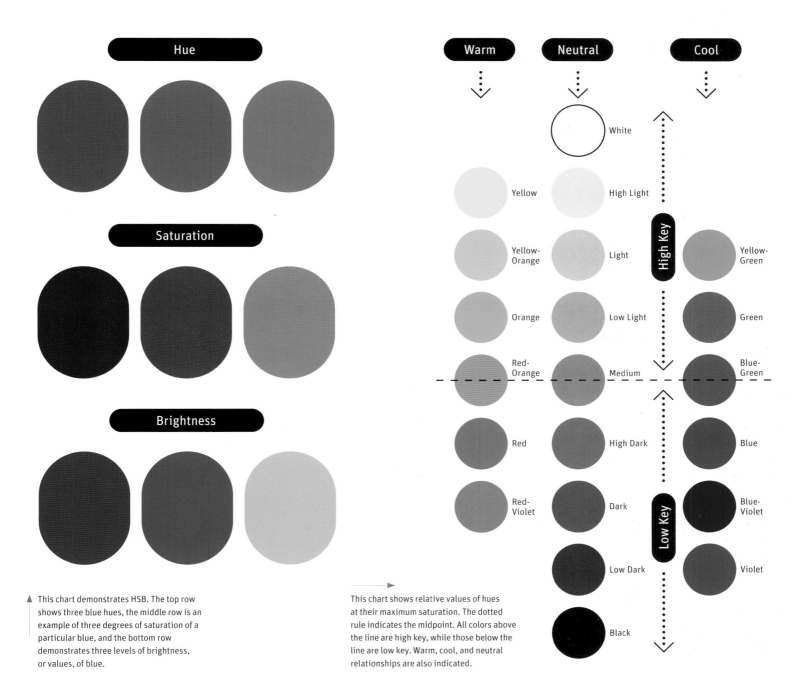

Hue

Saturation

Brightness

Warm   **Neutral**   **Cool**

White

Yellow   High Light

Yellow-   Light   Yellow-
Orange   Green

Orange   Low Light   Green

Red-   Medium   Blue-
Orange   Green

Red   High Dark   Blue

Red-   Dark   Blue-
Violet   Violet

               Low Dark   Violet

               Black

High Key

Low Key

This chart demonstrates HSB. The top row
shows three blue hues, the middle row is an
example of three degrees of saturation of a
particular blue, and the bottom row
demonstrates three levels of brightness,
or values, of blue.

This chart shows relative values of hues
at their maximum saturation. The dotted
rule indicates the midpoint. All colors above
the line are high key, while those below the
line are low key. Warm, cool, and neutral
relationships are also indicated.

▲ Rather than a traditional capabilities brochure showcasing high-profile client work, the designers created a visual journey through the creative process of Publicis, the U.S. branch of the world's third-largest communications company. This brochure boldly features Publicis' signature red almost exclusively in a series of unexpected visual relationships and verbal twists.
Carbone Smolan Agency

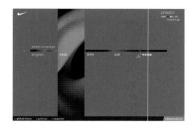

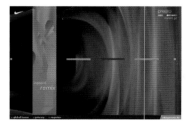

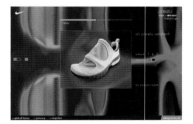

The colors and visual language for Nike Presto, a fashion product brand targeted toward trendsetting youth audiences in the Asia Pacific market, were born out of the collaboration of the firms Weiden + Kennedy Tokyo, Motion Theory, and Hello Design. The website has a high degree of music and color-driven interactivity. The graphics utilize the colors of the visible spectrum with vibrant dynamics meant to appeal to one of the most style-saturated corners of the world.
Hello Design

INTERNATIONAL DESIGN FORUM

BEIJING, CHINA
5.19–24. 2000

The poster for the 2000 International Biennial in Beijing, China, designed by Steff Geissbuhler, features a bright spectrum of colors that convey both internationalism and a sense of festivity. The rich blue background provides a dark field from which the other colors pop.
Chermayeff & Geismar

**Chapter 2:
Color Theory**

What Is Color Theory?

Color theory is a set of guiding principles that can be used to create harmonious color combinations. These ideas are represented in a variety of diagrams— color wheels, triangles, and charts that help designers understand color interactions, select and combine colors, and construct pleasing and effective palettes.

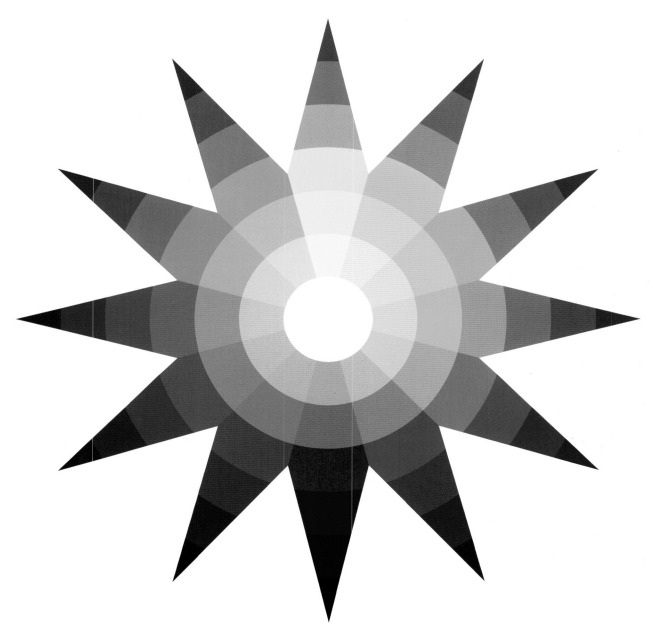

▲ Diagrams such as this color wheel, which shows pure hues as well as tints and shades, serve as a guide for selecting and combining colors beyond the pure hues. Different color theory diagrams have different purposes. Some are simple and some are complex, but all are useful references when thinking about color and choosing color palettes.

A Brief History of Color Theory

Many measurement systems, but all color theory has one goal: to explain color relationships with an aim to create harmony.

We offer this brief account to familiarize designers with the major color theorists and their significant findings. We encourage further exploration of this topic to gain a deeper understanding of color theory.

Since ancient times, color theorists have developed ideas and inter- pretations of color relationships. Attempts to formalize and recognize order date back at least to Aristotle (384–322 B.C.E.) but began in earnest with Leonardo da Vinci (1452–1519) and have progressed ever since. Leonardo noted that certain colors intensify each other, discovering *contrary* or *complementary* colors. The first color wheel was invented by Britain's Sir Isaac Newton (1642–1727), who split white light into red, orange, yellow, green, blue, indigo and violet beams, then joined the two ends of the spectrum to form a circle showing the natural progression of colors. When Newton created the color wheel, he noticed that mixing two colors from opposite positions produced a neutral or *anonymous* color.

More than a century later, while studying the psychological effects of color, Germany's famed poet and playwright Johann Wolfgang von Goethe (1749–1832) furthered color theory. Goethe divided all colors into two groups. On the plus side he put the warm colors (red to orange to yellow) and on the minus side the cool colors (green to blue to violet). He noted that colors on the plus side produced excitement in viewers, while he associated the minus-side colors with unsettled feelings. In 1810 Goethe published *Zur Farbenlehre* (*Theory of Color*), in which he disagreed with Newton's conclusions about color. He believed that a scien- tific approach alone did not enable one to fully understand color. Goethe's observations of the human perception of color, rather than just the physics of light, allowed him to discover important aspects of color theory, including simultaneous contrast and color's relationship to emotion.

Louis Prang (1824–1909) was an influential pioneer of American chromolithographs and a noted educator whose 1876 book *Theory of Color* helped popularize the theory of red, yellow, and blue primary colors in American art education. Wilhelm Ostwald (1853–1932), a Russian-German Nobel Prize–winning chemist, developed a color system related to psychological harmony and order in the 1916 *Die Farbenfibel* (*The Color Primer*). His ideas about color harmony influenced future color theorists and the Dutch de Stijl art movement (see page 100).

The next major set of theories comes from the Bauhaus, the highly influential German art and design school (1919–1933) that focused on the integration of art and industry, encouraging an ideology of functional design. Bauhaus member Johannes Itten (1888–1967) was a Swiss color and art theorist who developed *color chords* and modified the color wheel. Itten's color wheel is based on a primary triad of red, yellow, and blue, and includes twelve hues. He studied color in terms of both design and science, and his experiments with light waves explored color relationships and visual effects. Following Goethe's lead, Itten delved into the psychological and spiritual aspects of color. His most important work, *The Art of Color,* is summarized in his treatise called *Itten: The Elements of Color.* Itten's theories still form the core of most art school color information.

Josef Albers (1888–1976) studied under Itten and also taught at the Bauhaus. His abstract art used mathematical proportions to achieve balance and unity. After immigration to the United States, his teachings at Yale University led to his book *Interaction of Color,* a crucial text on color theory. Albers' focus is on what happens when colors interact, and his experiments are a resource for creating subtle color compositions. Faber Birren (1900–1988) explored the relationship between color and expression. His research helped clarify the historical development of the triadic color system.

The American artist Albert Munsell (1858–1918) created a new and versatile color model around 1905. Munsell was inspired by the work of fellow American Nicholas Ogden Rood (1831–1902) and German painter Philip Otto Runge (1777–1810) to develop a three-dimensional color model that demonstrates relationships between full-spectrum hues as well as tints and shades. Munsell's important realization was that, when pure, some hues are more saturated than others, so color relationships are distorted when forced into a circle. He created what is known as the Munsell Tree, with hues arranged along branches of different lengths in order of saturation. Munsell's work was adopted by American industry as its material standard for naming colors. It has also influenced the color-space modeling of the CIE (Commission International de l'Eclairge).

Artists, scientists, and scholars continue to contribute to color theory, a dynamic and fascinating subject.

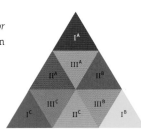

▲ The Goethe color triangle is an equilateral triangle subdivided into nine equi- lateral triangles. The three primary colors (blue is I^A, and so on) are arranged on the outer edges, with sec- ondary (purple is II^A, and so on) and tertiary (lavender is III^A, and so on) colors located inside. This is one method Goethe used to dem- onstrate color relationships. He believed that colors are linked to emotion, and his diagram demonstrates these connections. For example, he called I^C, II^C, III^C, and II^A a serene color scheme. Here again, the designation is completely subjective, as is true in nearly all color theories.

The Munsell Color Tree, when shown as a wheel (right), is divided into five primary or principal hues (R stands for red, y for yellow, etc.). Five intermediaries are also labeled with the initials of the surrounding principals (YR for yellow-red, etc.), producing a total of ten divisions. For even more accurate specification, the circle is divided into steps numbered clockwise from 5, at the top, to 100. This diagram is useful because it explains the rationale behind the Munsell color notation system. Designers may need to use the Munsell color notation system when specifying colors in manufacturing processes such as packaging and environmental design projects.

Johannes Itten held that color harmony was subjective. However, he developed a series of diagrams, such as these, for the construction of harmonious triads (three-color combinations, near right) and tetrads (four-color combinations, middle) in twelve-part color wheels. These groups of hues relate in pleasing ways. Spinning the center triangles or rectangles provides other successful combinations. His twelve-pointed star (far right) expands on the idea of a color wheel by showing hues along with tints and shades. The color star (right) is a more complex diagram of color interactions.

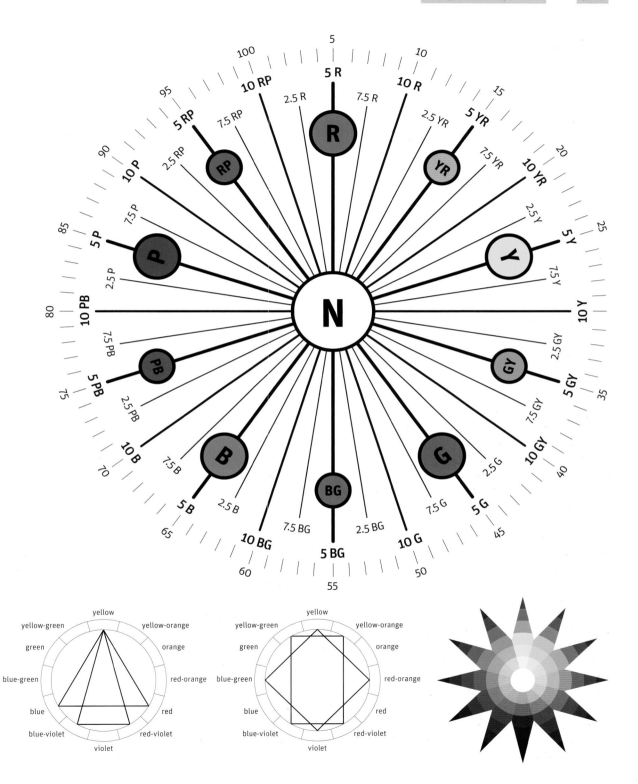

Color theory is, at its core, about developing aesthetically pleasing color relationships.

One of the best tools for visualizing color relationships is the color wheel. This wheel, originally developed by Sir Isaac Newton, can be constructed with just a few colors, or can be quite complex incorporating many color variations. Perhaps the most useful version is the twelve-step color wheel containing twelve equidistant pure hues, as shown below.

Successful color relationships can be referred to as "color harmonies." Whether they consist of similar hues that are soothing to the eye or are made of contrasting ones that excite the eye, color harmonies are often subject to personal preference. However, the study of art and design has given us some specific color theories, or guiding principles, that help us make effective decisions about color usage.

We recommend the use of the color wheel called the Subtractive Artists' Primary Colors (RYB), because picking colors is easiest with this set of primaries. The color wheel will help to select color combinations that balance each other. This balance is a result of all the colors in a chosen composition adding up to gray, or neutrality, in the eye/brain. This result will cause the work to just "feel right" to the viewer.

A color by itself will elicit an emotional and physical response, but the nature of the response can be altered by placing it in context with one or more colors. Color perceptions shift dynamically when aligned with other colors. Designers can vary color combinations to produce relationships that are allied or contrasting and therefore can affect viewers' impression.

12 Step Color Wheel

red · red orange · orange · orange yellow · yellow · yellow green · green · green blue · blue · blue purple · purple · purple red

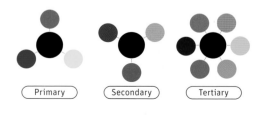

Primary   Secondary   Tertiary

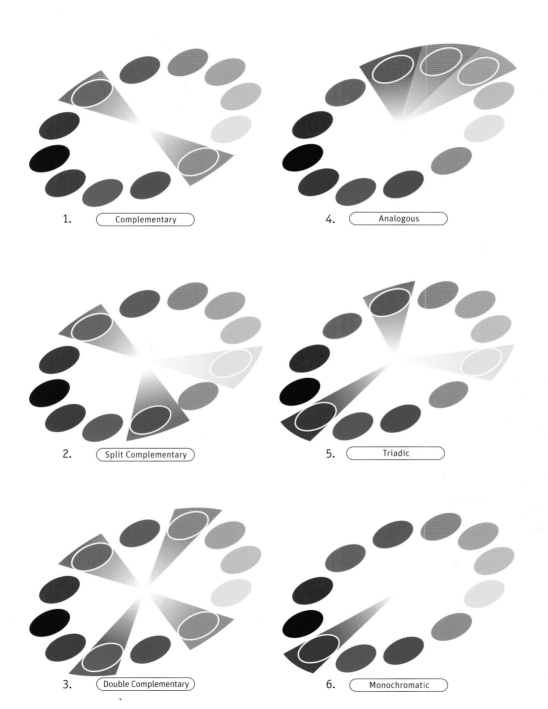

1. Complementary

2. Split Complementary

3. Double Complementary

4. Analogous

5. Triadic

6. Monochromatic

Color Harmony

Here are six basic color relationship concepts that can be applied to an infinite number of color combinations.

Complementary

1. These are color pairs that are directly opposite each other on the color wheel. They represent the most contrasting relationships. The use of two complementary colors will cause a visual vibration and excite the eye.

Split Complementary

2. These are the three-color schemes in which one color is accompanied by two others that are spaced equally from the first color's complement. The contrast is toned down somewhat, providing a more sophisticated relationship.

Double Complementary

3. This is the combination of two pairs of complementary colors. As complements increase the apparent intensity of each other, not all color sets will be pleasing. Avoid using equal volumes of the four colors to make the scheme less jarring.

Analogous

4. These are combinations of two or more colors that are spaced equally from each other on the color wheel. These colors have similar light ray wavelengths, so they are easiest on the eye.

Triadic

5. These are combinations of any three colors that are spaced evenly around the color wheel. Triads with primaries are garish, but secondary and tertiary triads provide softer contrast. Triads in which two of the colors share a common primary (e.g., purple and orange share red) may seem more pleasing.

Monochromatic

6. These are color schemes made up of shades and tints of a single color. Use one hue and explore variety in saturation and lightness to form an allied combination of similar colors.

The packaging of the music CD series *Elemental Chill* has a beautiful palette of sophisticated muted colors in orange, red, green, and blue. When selecting a color scheme, it is important to consider the use of tints and shades of hues in order to create a pleasing and harmonious balance in the color system. Referring to color theory diagrams such as Itten's color star shown on page 16 allows designers to visualize color interactions.
Karlsson Wiliker

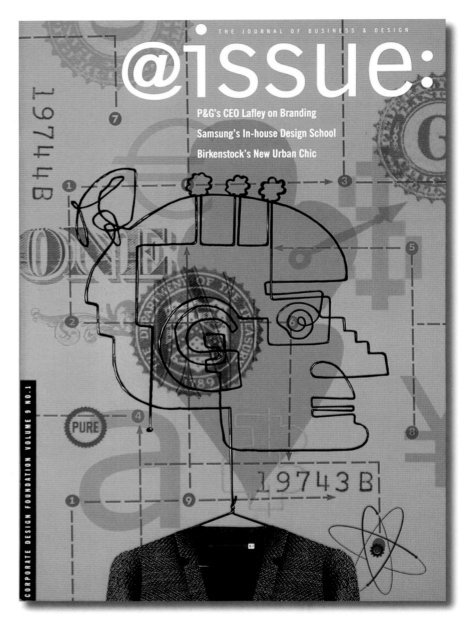

This cover for *@ISSUE: The Journal of Business and Design,* published by Sappi Fine Paper and the Corporate Design Foundation, utilizes a predominantly analogous composition of orange and red with bits of black and gray. The design is complemented by a desaturated green symbol acting as a central punctuation in the design.
Pentagram

The Cook's Canon

101 Classic Recipes Everyone Should Know

RAYMOND SOKOLOV

The *Cook's Canon* cookbook demonstrates a clever use of a classic complementary color scheme of orange and blue. Michael Hodgson designed the dust jacket in predominantly reflex blue, while the book cover itself is its opposite, orange. Using hues that are complements provide the most color contrast possible; the result is maximum excitement to the eye.
Ph.D

Chapter 3:
Color Meanings

The human eye and brain experience color physically, mentally, and emotionally. As a result, colors themselves have meanings. Color symbolism is often a cultural agreement, and opinions about the associations are varied and sometimes conflicting.

The Color Index charts on the following pages provide a sampling of color meanings, associations, and anecdotal information about color. Be sure to investigate a particular color's meanings and associations before using it in a design project.

Color Index

Primary

	Color	Associated with	Positive	Negative
	Red	fire blood sex	passion love blood energy enthusiasm excitement heat power	aggression anger battle revolution cruelty immorality
	Yellow	sunshine	intellect wisdom optimism radiance joy idealism	jealousy cowardice deceit caution
	Blue	sea sky	knowledge coolness peace masculinity contemplation loyalty justice intelligence	depression coldness detachment apathy

Cultural links	In addition	Sample
Ivory Coast, Africa Dark red indicates death. **France** Masculinity **Most of Asia** Marriage, prosperity, happiness **India** Soldier's symbol **South Africa** Color of mourning	• Most visually dominant color • Suggests speed, action • Stimulates heart rate, breathing, and appetite • People appear heavier in red clothes. • Red cars are stolen most often.	 This souvenir tour book was created for the singer Cher's Farewell Concert Tour. Pictured here is the back cover of the book on which the color red predominates to convey the passionate, spicy side of Cher. Color is manipulated to feature a variety of reds. **Chase Design Group**
Buddhist cultures Priests wear saffron yellow robes. **Egypt and Burma** Signifies mourning **India** Symbol of merchant or farmer **Hindu cultures** Worn to celebrate the festival of spring **Japan** Associated with courage	• First color that the human eye notices • Brighter than white • Speeds the metabolism • Bright yellow is the most fatiguing color; can irritate the eyes. • Pale yellow can enhance concentration (used for legal pads).	 The cover of the *American Photography 17* book, featuring bright yellow with a hint of red, virtually shouts to pass-ersby—the goal of the designer. The back cover is the reverse of the front, with red dominating the yellow. *AP17* is a handsome 432-page volume that presents the best photography of the year, as selected by a jury of publishing professionals. **344 Design**
Most of the world Considered a masculine color **China** Color for little girls **Iran** Color of mourning **Western bridal tradition** Means love **Worldwide** Most popular corporate color	• Blue food is rare in nature; unappetizing, suppresses hunger. • Causes the body to produce calming chemicals; relaxing • People are said to be more productive in blue rooms. • Blue clothing often symbolizes loyalty or trust.	 The front cover of Cher's souvenir tour book illustrates Cher's cool serene side with its blue tones. The designers used similar photos of Cher in both covers but altered them with color changes to develop the naughty and nice themes. **Chase Design Group**

Color Index

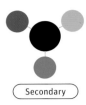

Secondary

	Color	Associated with	Positive	Negative
	Green	plants the natural environment	fertility money growth healing success nature harmony honesty youth	greed envy nausea poison corrosion inexperience
	Purple	royalty spirituality	luxury wisdom imagination sophistication rank inspiration wealth nobility mysticism	exaggeration excess madness cruelty
	Orange	autumn citrus	creativity invigoration uniqueness energy vibrancy stimulation sociability health whimsy activity	crassness trendiness loudness

Cultural links	In addition	Sample
Islam Green is associated with paradise and is symbolic of Islam. **Ireland** Green is strongly associated with this country. **Celtic cultures** The Green Man was the god of fertility. **Native American cultures** Green is linked with the will, or man's volition.	• Green is the easiest color on the eyes. • Green is a calming and refreshing color, often used in hospitals to relax patients. • Green means "go"; everything is in order. • Green is said to aid digestion and reduce stomachaches.	 The U.S. Environmental Protection Agency (EPA) is dedicated to protecting human health and the environment. The obvious choice for the identity was a bright grass green to signify nature. **Chermayeff & Geismar**
Latin America Purple indicates death. **Thailand** Purple is worn by widows mourning a husband's death. **Japan** Purple represents ceremony, enlightenment, and arrogance.	• Purple has a feminine and romantic quality that is sometimes associated with male homosexuality. • Rare in nature, purple seems artificial. • In ancient times, purple dyes were expensive and worn by royalty and the wealthy only. • Purple is said to enhance the imagination and thus is used in decorating children's rooms.	 Encounter Restaurant is located in the 1960s futuristic "Theme Building" at Los Angeles International Airport. The logo, a deep intense violet to mirror the exterior lighting feature that plays across the building's exterior, sparks the imagination about the future. **AdamsMorioka**
Ireland Orange signifies the Protestant movement in Northern Ireland. **Native American cultures** Orange is linked with learning and kinship. **India** Orange signifies Hinduism. **Netherlands** Orange is the national color because the Dutch monarchs came from Orange-Nassau.	• Orange is an appetite stimulant. • Orange rooms get people thinking and talking. • Orange rooms speak of friendliness and fun. • Orange is used for visibility enhancement, which is why hunters and highway workers wear it.	 The Nickelodeon kids' TV network identity was originally designed by Tom Corey and utilizes white balloon type knocked out of any orange shape. Orange was chosen because it was little used in children's products at that time and because the color is a bit irreverent, which captured Nick's point of view. This electron logo is a new version of the classic in irreverent orange. **AdamsMorioka**

Color Index

Neutral

	Color	Associated with	Positive	Negative
	Black	night death	power authority weight sophistication elegance formality seriousness dignity solitude mystery stylishness	fear negativity evil secrecy submission mourning heaviness remorse emptiness
	White	light purity	perfection marriage/wedding cleanliness virtue innocence lightness softness sacredness simplicity truth	fragility isolation
	Gray	neutrality	balance security reliability modesty classicism maturity intelligence wisdom	lack of commitment uncertainty moodiness cloudiness old age boredom indecision bad weather sadness

Cultural links	In addition	Sample
China Black is for little boys. **Asia generally** Black is associated with career, knowledge, mourning and penance. **American, European, Japanese youth** Black is the color of rebellion. **Worldwide** Black denotes dark-skinned people of sub-Saharan African ancestry.	• Black clothing makes people look thinner. • Black humor is morbid. • Black makes other colors look brighter. • In color therapy, black is supposed to boost self-confidence and strength. • Black is often associated with secret societies.	This L.A. Louver Gallery catalog for artist Richard Dievenkorn's black and white pencil drawings was given a black cover to suggest the exhibition works as well as to provide dignified elegance. **AdamsMorioka**
Japan and China White is a funeral color. **Worldwide** A white flag is a universal symbol for truce. **North America, Europe** White denotes light-skinned people of Caucasian ancestry. **India** Married women who wear white invite unhappiness.	• In some culture, it's considered good luck to be married in a white garment. • White is the perfectly balanced color. • White is so brilliant that it gives some people headaches. • White light can be blinding. • White is associated with angels and gods.	Minimal graphic elements, primarily the design firm's logo, against a stark white background create a feeling of open space while being a self-promotion that celebrates the new year in this 2002 poster. **344 Design**
Native American Gray is associated with honor and friendship. **Asian** Gray means helpful people as well as travel. **America** The color gray is used to represent industry, in contrast to environmentalism, which is represented by green. **Worldwide** Gray is often associated with silver and money.	• Gray seldom evokes strong emotions. • Gray is a balance of black and white. • Gray is its own complement. • Grayscale means rendering an image in a range of blacks and whites. It also refers to a tonal scale of blacks and whites that is used in calibration and accurate reproduction of halftone images.	This promo for fashion designer Anni Kuan features New York Laundromats. The gray effect is achieved by printing black ink on newsprint. The overall effect of the piece is a balanced yet gritty portrait of the city rendered in monochromatic images. **Sagmeister, Inc**

The Richard Diebenkorn sample catalog reads:

Richard Diebenkorn
Drawing from the model 1954–1967

L A LOUVER

Chapter 4:

10

Rules of Color

There really are no right or wrong ways to use color. Some color design processes and color combinations work better than others, but there are many ways to achieve great results. We offer these ten rules as a way to approach color. The rules incorporate physics, theory, psychology, economics, aesthetics, and usage in order to effectively harness this powerful design element.

1. Convey information.

2. Create color harmony.

3. Attract and hold attention.

4. Remember that context is everything.

5. Consider that experimentation is key.

6. Know that people see color differently.

7. Assist in mnemonic value.

8. Think about composition.

9. Use standardized color systems.

10. Understand limitations.

① Convey Information

The Right Color sends the Right Message

Color has the ability to evoke a response, create a mood, symbolize an idea, and express an emotion. Differences in particular aspects of color, such as a change in value or intensity, can further refine a color's tone and meaning. People have their own associations with color, but there are conscious and subconscious social and cultural connotations too. Every color has its own set of connections that convey information, with the color itself acting as a signifier of ideas—both positive and negative. (See Color Meaning, Chapter 3.)

Sources of Color Meanings

All color meanings are relative; these interpretations are influenced by a variety of factors, including age, gender, personal experience, mood, ethnic identity, history, and tradition. Affinity for the particular colors of a nation's flag shows how tradition, nationalism, and history impact color responses.

Color preferences that predominate when a person comes of age (or nostalgia for a particular time in history) can cause resonance. For example, the earth-tone palette of harvest gold, avocado green, and burnt orange—central to 1970s color schemes— evokes strong associations in people who were teenagers then.

Color assignment based on gender, as in the Western tradition of pink for girls and blue for boys, is both adopted and subverted in children's products. However, it is rare for male-oriented objects to be colored pink in any culture. Are such differences between the sexes due to physiology or socialization? No one is quite sure, but a recent study found that

The color scheme of red and black supports the passionate emotional content of the play *Fucking A* which is promoted in this New York Public Theater poster designed by Paula Scher and Sean Carmody. *Fucking A* is Suzan-Lori Park's contemporary reshaping of the classic novel *The Scarlet Letter*. Today, the *A* stands for abortion rather than for adultery. Wearing red letters was a public source of shame in colonial America, and the designers employ this concept and color convention in the poster for the play.
Pentagram Design, Ltd.

More than just a visual phenomenon, color has emotional and cultural dimensions that can enhance—or impede— communication efforts.

more women than men have a favorite color. Also, when asked for a preference between bright and soft colors, women tend to pick soft colors while men choose bright ones.

Age is another important factor related to color interpretation. Children and the elderly have an affinity for intense, bright colors. Teenagers like whatever their parents don't appreciate. In addition, a 1976 study showed the effects of color on mood. Groups of people were placed in different rooms— one colorful and complex, the other gray and sterile. Researchers recorded pulse rates as well as individuals' subjective emotional feelings. The results showed stress and boredom in the gray room, supporting the notion that color causes both physical and emotional responses, all of which could trigger judgments about specific colors.

Tapping into Color's Associations

Psychologists have suggested that color impression can account for as much as 60 percent of the acceptance or rejection of a product or service. When choosing colors to enhance the message being communicated, it is essential to anticipate audience perceptions. All color is relative, and people can have strong, often subconscious, prejudices against certain colors and color schemes.

It is a designer's job to select colors that elicit correct responses. They need to consider carefully for whom a piece is being created, and how internal and external audiences will read the design in terms of color alone. It's not just an aesthetic choice. Designers need to leverage color meaning to achieve their client's goals.

▲ In this promotional poster for a lecture given by Sean Adams, the designer uses an image of the American flag as a prominent visual device. Since many people have the perception of AdamsMorioka as being the "All-American" design firm, the poster leverages that concept while gently lampooning it, using both color and imagery that echoes the theme.
AdamsMorioka

Shown here is a representative sample of flags from countries around the world. Designers can take cues from these color palettes to create affinity, as well as discord, with their designs. Nationalism is often strongly associated with flag colors and is therefore a key factor in inherent color meaning for many people.

Afghanistan | Iran
Argentina | Netherlands
Australia | Ireland
Bahamas | Israel
Brazil | Japan
Canada | Mexico
China | Russia
Cuba | South Africa
France | Spain
Germany | Sweden
United Kingdom | Turkey
Greece | Tibet
India | USA

"Research reveals that all human beings make an unconscious judgment about a person, environment, or item within ninety seconds of initial viewing and that between 62 percent and 90 percent of that assessment is based on color alone."—The Institute for Color Research

▲ The Blue Bar is the lounge in the Berkeley, a luxury hotel in Knightsbridge, London. Given the name, the obvious color choice for the graphics is blue. The color evokes various musical references as well, from "Blue Note Jazz" to "singing the blues" to "blue suede shoes." A cool blue hue adds a sophisticated edge to this promotional music CD package that mimics a matchbook.
Pentagram

Is there a difference in the way males and females respond to and interpret color? Yes. Some of the research leads us to wonder whether it is nature or nurture; regardless, the gender of the intended audience is an important factor to consider when choosing a color palette for any design project.

A 1934 study found evidence that the most pleasing color combinations were obtained from either very small or very large differences in hue, rather than medium differences. These were more frequently preferred by females than males. Based on this information, perhaps females can discern more differences in colors than males.

Home Shopping Network is a retail shopping television network, a virtual on-air catalog offering everything from housewares to jewelry to clothing items. Color is used to draw in the target audience of twenty- to fifty-year-old women. The pastel palette creates a friendly yet subtly stimulating visual experience to persuade buyers to act immediately and make a purchase. The color scheme is similar to those found in many physical retail environments in which the target audience is used to shopping, therefore allowing the customer to make a direct association with previous purchasing experiences.
AdamsMorioka

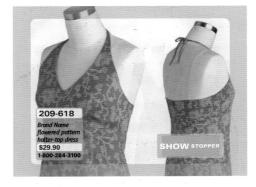

Creative director Yu Tsai chose blocks of vibrant color anchored by a cool neutral grey for the branding of Decor, a furniture manufacturing company with a thoroughly modern approach. Inspired by swatches of fabrics and the detailed process of stitching, the designers created a colorful identity system that illustrates and emphasizes Decor's style: minimalist and classy.
88 Phases

The colors—orange, pale and reflex blues, and a yellow-olive green—are arranged in squares that excite the eye and suggest special arrangements, such as floor plans. Orange, prominently used for Decor, is associated with youthful energy and chic sophistication.
88 Phases

In a 1959 study, researchers found that males were generally more tolerant of achromatic colors (colors with zero saturation and, therefore, no hue, such as neutral grays, white, or black) than females were. This led researchers to propose that females might be more color-conscious as well as more flexible and diverse in their color preferences.

Researchers also found in a 1990 study that females are more likely than males to have a favorite color. When asked whether they preferred light versus dark colors, there were no significant differences between males and females. However, when asked to choose between bright or soft colors, the females preferred soft colors, while the males

preferred the bright ones. What is the favorite color of each gender? There is no one answer—research seems to provide conflicting results. Another study of color identification and vocabulary was done with college students in 1995. Students were asked to look at and identify twenty-one different color chips. Females recognized significantly more

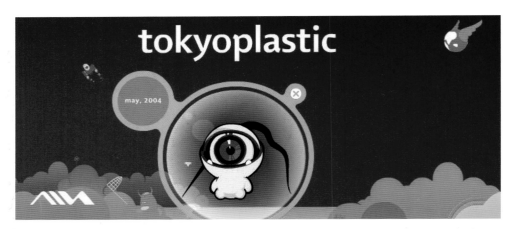

When Aiwa became a subsidiary of Sony Corporation, the consumer electronics brand repositioned itself to create stylish and innovative audio/video products for the youth market. Hello Design, in partnership with Weiden + Kennedy, The_Groop, and Oceanmonsters, designed and developed Aiwaworld TV, the main portion of Aiwaworld to serve up audiovisual "hybrid music."

Above are four screens featuring the colorful animated world created for Aiwaworld TV. The designers used a parallax engine to create a 3-D experience in which users can explore a topsy-turvy world inspired by Japanese pop culture. A bright palette of colors echoes the comic book references,

working to fully immerse the viewer in a kinder, more fun-filled world. No dominant color is used to convey a particular message in Aiwaworld TV; rather, it is a collection of colors taken from the Japanese anime genre, which has a youthful voice. The colors work to invite the viewer into a familiar yet new kind of storytelling.

Aiwaworld TV not only complements existing Aiwaworld content but also provides an engaging experience that speaks to young audiences, creating a unique brand impression for the client.
Hello Design

elaborate colors than the males did. Findings also indicated that the differences in responses to color identification might be attributed to a difference in the way males and females are socialized.

"Colors are the mother tongue of the subconscious."—Carl Jung

Using Proprietary Colors to Convey Information

The idea of "owning" a color is one of the highest priorities in managing logos and corporate identities and is generally important to all design and advertising visual systems. Orange has been associated with the children's television network Nickelodeon for almost two decades. Pantone 659, a deep, dark blue, is used in the identity system of retail clothing giant The Gap and was also the name of one of the company's fragrance products. In these cases, color creates a symbolic link with the producer and its products. A bright golden yellow has been associated with photographic products manufacturer Kodak for decades. The color becomes a stand-in for the concepts of "kids' entertainment" or "trendy clothing" or even arguably, "photography."

Perhaps subverting standard meanings would help to make a color proprietary. What if a health-related product had a black or brown logo instead of the expected green one? Would organic food packaging jump off the shelf more if it were designed in unnatural, even day-glo, colors? What about a slick, high-tech company adopting an earthy organic color palette? All of these could separate a brand from its competition. Most clients would relish the idea of having color alone symbolize their company.

Color as a Convention

Color meanings are held deep in our subconscious. Color is a state of mind as much as anything. In a physical sense, there is no such thing as color, just light waves of different wavelengths. The human eye can distinguish between the wavelengths, so we see the world in color. However, the human brain perceives more. We *feel* color. It has biological, psychological, social, and cultural dimensions, all of which give it meaning and convey information.

Pale blue dominates this poster promoting the Spring Lecture Series at the Southern California Institute of Architecture (Sci-Arc), a leading-edge school of experimental architecture. The simple criteria was to incorporate the Latin prefix *re*—as in *rethink*, *reinvent*, *redefine*—so the designers played with the notion of everything coming full circle in the graphics. Organic shapes in delicate blue, overlaid by bold black typography and punctuated by bits of red and yellow, illustrate that an atypical color palette can effectively convey bold ideas. The die-cut square in the center of the poster even allows the viewer to recontextualize the graphics themselves.
88 Phases

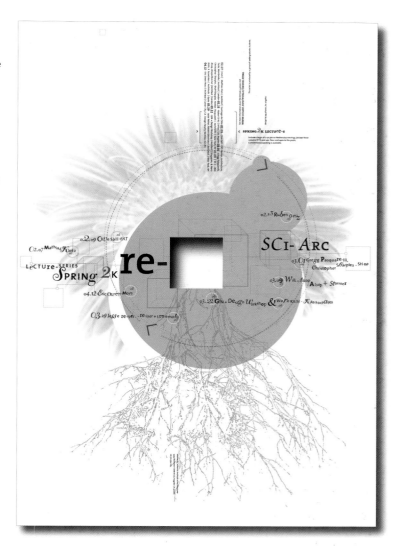

② Create Color Harmony

To a certain extent, pleasing color harmony is just like any other aspect of beauty: it is in the eye of the beholder. What is pleasing to one person may not be pleasing to another. Color harmony nevertheless is related to the organizing principles of all artwork: balance, variety, proportion, dominance, movement, rhythm, and repetition. These are some of the traditional metrics for determining whether or not a piece, be it fine art or graphic design, is pleasing and works.

Making Color Choices

Keeping this in mind, designers need to select the colors for each and every project carefully. Some of their decisions may be based on their own preferences, while others may be heavily influenced by client input and preferences. Selecting inventive combinations of hues, along with specific tints and shades, is a practiced skill. The more you do it, the better you get.

Most designers seek a color scheme that engages the viewer and provides a balanced visual experience. The deliberate avoidance of harmony must be viewed as a means of inducing an agitated or chaotic reaction in the viewer. Designers must decide in what direction they are headed and for what reason. The starting point for all decisions about color harmony comes down to a creative interpretation of the message that needs to be communicated. What combination of colors will best convey the desired meaning? If those colors are clichéd and overused, what are the best alternatives? Can the effect be refined by a slight modification of color choice?

Adfusion is a company providing an emarketplace for media acquisition professionals. The corporate identity colors reflect energy and sophistication and allow for flexibility of application with its palette of five colors. Pure orange and red are used in conjunction with intermediary hues of yellow-green, blue-violet, and blue-green.
Robert Bynder Design

Harmony is a factor of cohesion—the pleasing relationships among graphic elements, especially color.

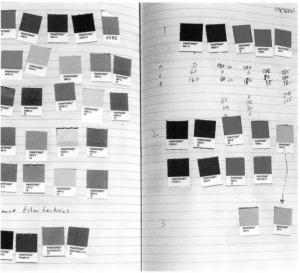

Sean Adams keeps a journal of color palettes as an easy reference guide to color schemes. At left, see pages for the Sundance Film Festival and the California Institute of the Arts (CalArts) color palettes. This logbook of ideas includes approved and unapproved color palettes and serves as a creative resource for thinking about color in all types of projects. **AdamsMorioka**

PANTONE Colors displayed here may not match the PANTONE-identified standards. Consult current PANTONE Color Publications for accurate color. PANTONE® and the PANTONE Chip Logo® are the property of Pantone, Inc.

Eight Rules for Building a Color Palette

The following steps are recommended for creating timeless color schemes that are effective in all media and for all cultures. The steps are based on the research of Professor Hideaki Chijiwa, Musashino Bijutsu Daigaku (Musashino University of Fine Arts), in the book *Color Harmony: A Guide to Creative Color Combinations* (Rockport Publishers).

1. Figure out the purpose.
Think about why you are choosing a color palette and for what kind of client. Investigate color meanings and associations.

2. Review color basics.
Make sure you have reviewed basics such as hue, saturation, intensity, and the ways in which colors affect each other in relationship. Study layouts you like to analyze possible palettes for the current project.

3. Choose a dominant color, then accent colors.
Decide on an overall background color, or color for the largest areas, first. Then select possible accent colors. Sometimes the accent color is fixed. For example, a client may have a corporate color that must be used. In that case, keep the accent color in mind when selecting the dominant color.

4. Select shades, then vary them.
Because the shade of a color heavily impacts the overall impression, decide what feeling must be conveyed—bright and cheery, or perhaps serene and dignified. Note that colors of the same hue but of varying shades and tints can look very different and still remain harmonious. Varying the shades of hues to create contrast of light and dark can be effective and dramatic.

5. Look at compatibility of hues.
Having selected a preliminary color scheme and considered a variety of tints and shades, look at the overall compatibility of colors. Is the contrast pleasing? If not, go back to refine the palette with intermediate hues. For example, with green selected as the dominant color, perhaps red-orange would work better than pure red.

6. Limit the number of colors.
With a palette now chosen, review the number of colors. Two or three colors are usually enough. Four must be chosen with care, while five might be too many. Sometimes budget limitations as well as aesthetic considerations narrow the palette.

7. Put the colors into action.
Put the colors to use in a few typical pieces required by the client. Look at how they work together. If the color palette is successful, your designs will be harmonious. If not, further refinements are warranted.

8. Keep a logbook.
Once you have found color palettes that work, document them in a journal. Paste in color chips and include the client's name and a project description. The logbook will serve as a reference when choosing future color palettes.

Combining Colors

The science of color harmony involves the categorization and determination of the dynamic symmetry in color groupings. Effectively doing so goes back to understanding and utilizing color theory to create color relationships such as complements, split complements, triads, analogies, monochromatics, and the like. (Please see Chapter 2.) Color science becomes art when a designer knows how to use colors, in what proportions, and for what purpose, to create a desired response.

Designers know that contrast intensifies color. Fully saturated colors create a lively impression. White and black alter the perception of other colors. Different types of color schemes have different positive and negative factors. For example, analogous color schemes (adjacent hues on the color wheel) are soothing to the eye and easy to create but lack contrast and vibrancy. Split complementary color schemes (a hue plus the two hues adjacent to its complement) are more sophisticated and nuanced than complementary color schemes (two hues directly opposite on the color wheel). Split complements have a strong visual impact but can be difficult to balance. Triadic color schemes (three hues equally spaced around the color wheel) offer contrast, but less contrast than a complementary scheme. Tetradic, or double complementary color schemes (two pairs of complementary hues), are the richest schemes with the most variety but are by far the hardest to balance. Monochromatic color schemes (variations in tints and shades of a single hue) are clean and elegant but lack contrast and often lack impact as well.

Naturally, there are always exceptions. Talented, creative people can take delight in stretching the boundaries of what works in color schemes. Color harmony fascinates designers. Experimenting with it allows them to develop their unique point of view. Color interactions are both optical and aesthetic phenomena. Designers must formulate a process for visualizing color combinations that allows them to shift with changing media, clients, and trends in color usage.

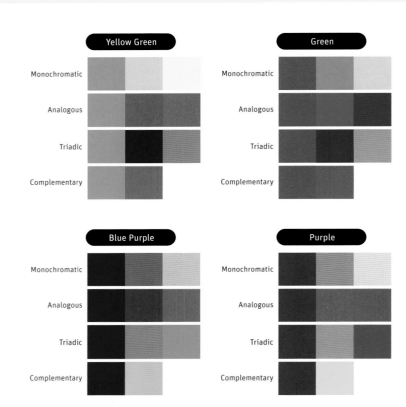

"Besides a balance through color harmony, which is comparable
to symmetry, there is equilibrium between color tensions,
related to a more dynamic equilibrium." —Josef Albers

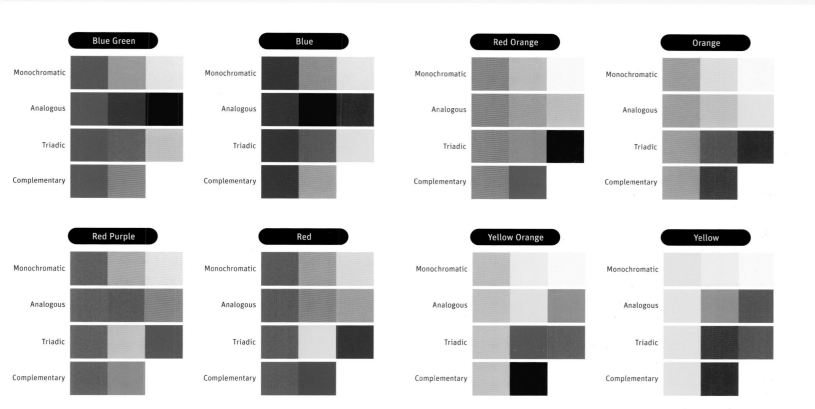

Color Harmony Chart

Shown here is a reference guide for creating pleasing color harmonies. Included for each of the hues of the twelve-step color wheel is an example of a monochromatic, analogous, triadic, and complementary color scheme. These samples can be used as a reminder of possible color combinations when beginning the process of building a color scheme for a project. Color harmony is often a fusion of the fundamentals of color physics tempered by aesthetic practice. Color can be used to dazzle, soothe, charm, irritate, agitate, or annoy—all through the choice of specific relationships.

Color on a Biological Level
Chromotherapy, or color therapy, is a practice that uses the seven colors of the rainbow spectrum to promote health and healing. It is based on the premise that certain colors are infused with certain specific healing energies.

Color has played a role in healing for different cultures. In ancient Egypt, people were treated in rooms designed specifically to refract the sun's rays into different colors of the visible spectrum. Practitioners of Ayurveda, especially in India, believe that specific colors correspond with each of the seven chakras, or energy centers, of the body.

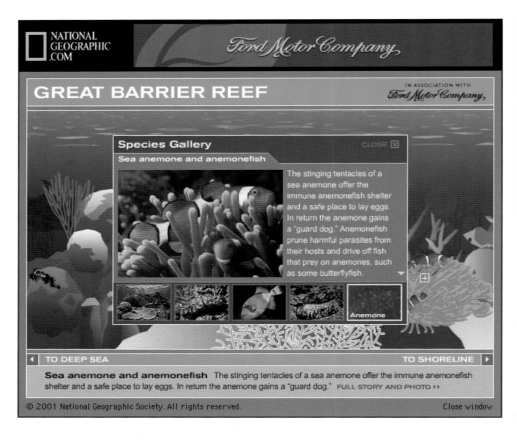

The website designs shown here are great examples of color harmony in practice. The National Geographic's *Earth Pulse* website, by Hello Design (left), uses an analogous color scheme featuring blues and greens that perfectly capture an undersea mood. The *Retrogurgitation* website, designed by Michele Moore Graphic Design (opposite, top left), is an entertainment site about the return of fashion trends. The site utilizes a complementary color scheme of red and green. Singer-songwriter Kirstin Candy's website, also by Moore (opposite, top right), uses a predominantly monochromatic palette of blue-violets to theatrically offset the color portraits of the artist. Moore's design for John Fogerty's website (opposite, lower right) effectively uses another analogous color scheme, this one with reds, golds, and oranges. The Michele Moore Graphic Design website home page (opposite, lower left) virtually eschews color by adopting a primarily black achromatic color scheme. This makes the minimalist white typography pop off the screen. In subpages on this site, the predominantly black color scheme allows full-color photos of the designer's work samples to stand out more vividly.
Hello Design • Michele Moore Graphic Design

Traditional Chinese medicine holds that each organ of the body is associated with a certain color. In Qigong, a self-healing art that combines movement and meditation, different organs and emotions are associated with both healing sounds and specific colors. Both practices use color to treat a wide variety of mental and physical imbalances.

In 1878, physician Edwin D. Babbitt (1828–1905) published *Principles of Light and Color,* in which he described his work on healing with colored lights. Dr. Dinshah P. Ghadiali (1873–1966) built on Babbitt's work, continuing to develop the practice of chromotherapy. Though controversial, Babbitt's work continues to inspire color therapists today.

Wearing specific colors, drinking colored water, meditating about a color, and being bathed in colored lights may all be relaxing. However, few clinical studies of color therapy have been conducted, which leaves open the question of whether or not chromatherapy is effective in treating disease.

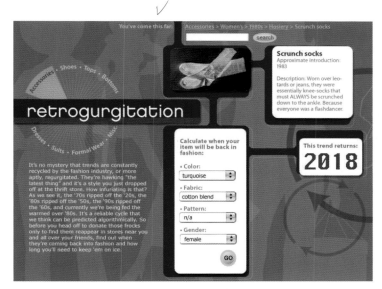

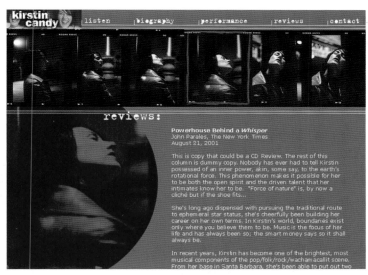

3   Attract and Hold Attention

As color is a visual language in and of itself, a designer can use it to attract the eye and focus attention on the intended messages in the work. Color can be used to irritate or relax, encourage participation or alienate—it is completely up to the designer. Josef Albers said, "Whether bright or dull, singular or complex, physiological or psychological, theoretical or experiential, the persuasive power of color attracts and motivates."

Color Physiology Influences Design

Strong visual statements can distinguish a designer's work and the client's message from the competition. Using physiological phenomena to get attention will also assist in this goal. Our brains and eyes participate with the designer to either accept or reject a particular design. As humans, we seek balance, especially in terms of color. For example, when exposed to a particular hue, our brains seem to expect the complementary color. If it is present, the combination looks vibrant. If it is absent, our brains tend to produce it to form a balance.

The eye naturally recognizes certain contrasts and colors, specifically the colors found in the rainbow spectrum. Perception of other colors, such as muted tertiary colors and tints and shades of spectrum hues, may require an intellectual shift to recognize. Since humans cannot see all possible colors, color perception is evoked by picking up on dominant wavelengths of spectral light. Dominant wavelength is the perceptual idea that gives us the concept of hue (e.g., if the dominant wavelength of an object is red, the object is perceived as being the color red). Therefore, the eye is nearly always drawn to what it can easily perceive. This is the scientific reason why a design utilizing primary colors attracts our attention instantly.

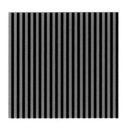

 This optical illusion is known as the McCollough Effect. Look at the colored grids, above, for a few minutes. Then look at the black and white grids. There should seem to be a green haze around the horizontal lines and a magenta haze around the vertical lines. The cause of this effect is unclear, but it involves our neurotransmitters. The McCollough Effect demonstrates that color and orientation are two sources of stimulation in humans. Designers must consider not only the particular colors they choose but also their physical relationships, which affect perception and attention. This effect also demonstrates how our eyes and brains seek the complements of colors by creating the sensation of them.

This poster for a performance of the Stockholm Improvisa-tional Theater attracts attention with a bold use of color and shape. The dark indigo-blue juxtaposed with a near-comple-mentary yellow-orange and white creates the optical illusion of depth. Playing with optical dimension, enhanced by color choice, allows designers to fascinate the eye and draw the viewer in.
Sweden Graphics

This chart shows the Munker-White Effect. Even though the blue bars are identical (see right), when surrounded by different colors such as white or black, they appear to be completely different hues. This optical illusion also demonstrates a method for obtaining the appearance of more colors in a layout.

Optical Illusions Can Affect Design

Fascinating insights into how humans perceive and interpret color can be gained by studying optical illusions. Although we don't have a complete model of the way color information gets processed by the eye and brain, scientific research offers glimpses of various phenomenon that can prove significant to our understanding of how color works in design compositions. Visualizations of certain color combinations often play tricks on us, as illustrated in the diagrams on these pages.

Many scientists have studied color, and their research can be helpful to creatives. Colors react to each other on many levels, so it is important for a designer to understand this and leverage it.

The Transparency Effect

A perceptual phenomenon that can add to color compositions in design, especially in terms of creating special illusions, is called the Transparency Effect.

In color mixing, designers seek relationships between colors by altering hues with each other to create a specific hue. When two hues are mixed to form a third, the resulting color resembles both. If placed between the original two, the new mixed hue will not only be harmonious, but will also give a surprising illusion of transparency.

In cases shown above, the original two colors (the left ones and the right ones) look like overlapped transparent sheets that form the new middle color. These types of optical phenomena can be utilized to draw the eye into a design by achieving harmony and concordance among all the colors present.

"One way to make yourself stand out from the crowd is by using color in ways nobody else thought of." —Josef Albers

The two versions of promotional postcards for Bossa:Nova , a DJ collective that produces music/dance club performances, designed by Stefan Bucher, illustrate the way a change in color palette can effect mood in design. Different people respond to different color schemes, drawing in music lovers of various types, as in the smooth analogous blue green or the more lively complementary versions below.

344 Design

Another example of the way color interactions alter perception and get attention are these two posters created for the annual Push advertising and design conference. Similar in design, each poster incorporates a bird taking flight from a branch as a metaphor for creative freedom. Yet the posters look quite different due to the number of colors used. The single desaturated gray-green has a more subtle impact than the bolder near-complementary scheme at left.

Brand Integration Group/ Ogilvy & Mather NY

Afterimaging

A Color Perception Phenomenon

Another interesting color perception phenomenon is called afterimaging. Every color has an opposite, or complement. It is possible to determine a color's complement just by using our eyes. The rods and cones in our eyes vary in sensitivity to different light and will fatigue after prolonged exposure to a hue. Once fatigued, we will perceive the complement of that hue when we look away.

You can try this for yourself. Look at the flag image for several minutes, then gaze at a white sheet—you are experiencing an afterimage. Now stare at the blue square below. After a few minutes, look at the small gray square to its left. You should be able to see a square of the blue's complement—orange.

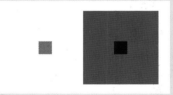

Afterimaging and other optical illusions are noteworthy because designers must understand that colors can significantly alter each other when juxtaposed.

Color and Human Emotion

Color is used in various forms of alternative medicine; color psychology is one example. This field, a relatively new area of research, is devoted to analyzing the effects that color has on human emotion. Some may call it a pseudoscience, but color psychology has its devotees worldwide.

Practitioners of color psychology, which is related to chromotherapy, note that many common physiological effects often accompany psychological responses to certain colors. However, variables such as age and cultural background may also affect responses.

Color can be used in a cityscape to attract attention. The large format banners for the BALTIC Centre for Contemporary Art in northern England are a striking combination of black and yellow. The color scheme evokes heavy industry as well as modern art.
blue river design

A bold red is used with the white of the stock in this poster to alert customers to Father's Day promotions at Boots, one of the United Kingdom's largest pharmacy chains. Red is one of the most visible colors in the spectrum. It stands out in any context and always demands attention.
Lippa Pearce

Color psychology is of particular significance to environmental graphic designers, whose color choices for installations and environments can greatly affect people's mood and actions. Color is an active influence on human consciousness.

Color has an impact on us because every cell in the body responds to light, and color is light. So we react to it, literally, on a cellular level. Color affects our bodies, our minds, and our moods.

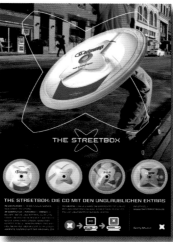

Based on research of a typical retail environment, color was used to differentiate a new line of Stanley automotive parts. In a strategic attempt to draw attention away from other products, a vivid burnt orange was chosen as the new core color for the brand.
Hornall Anderson Design Works

Here, vibrant primary colors are employed to cause the Sony StreetBox line of music products to stand out to German teenagers. Graphic treatments played against urban-inspired imagery and package formats work well because of the strong color palette.
Format Design

4 **Remember That Context Is Everything**

Color is always seen in context. Sometimes that context is proximity to another color, which alters its meaning or even the perception of the color itself. At other times the context is the environment surrounding the color—for example, the white of a page or the physical environment as a whole. The perception of color is always shifting, never fixed. All colors appear more brilliant when set against a black background. Conversely, they seem a bit duller on a white background. Complementary colors make each other appear brighter, yet the effect on the brain, when taken in total, is a balanced neutral gray. Certain color triadic schemes seem more garish or more sophisticated, more lively, or more sedate.

All Color Is Relative

The constant experimentation that occurs in the design process brings to light which colors are most pleasing to a particular designer's eyes. By understanding that all color is relative, designers can observe for themselves the effects colors have on each other. Sometimes a slight variation in tint or shade is enough to create the required emotional and aesthetic feeling.

Proximity to Other Colors

Optical color mixing, also referred to as *partitive color* or *simultaneous contrast,* is another important contextual phenomenon. This is the color perception that results from the combination of adjacent color areas by the eye and brain. Human perception mixes colors that are next to each other and forms a color impression based on the entire composition. The viewer may perceive colors that are not actually present. If it is imperative that a specific color is perceived first by the viewer, be sure to keep this phenomenon in mind.

A study in color contrasts—three different red squares, each with its own vertical column, are set on the same color backgrounds—white, red, green, and black. Note how the colors shift in relation to each other. Colors mutually influence each other, altering perception. Provocative color effects can be achieved with very slight variations in hue, as demonstrated here.

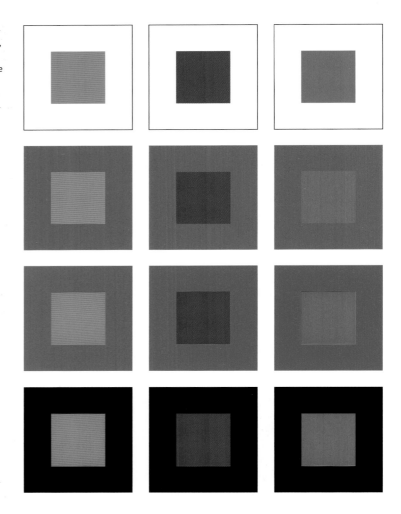

"A color has many faces."—Josef Albers

In addition, a hue's position on the color wheel can affect the perception of other hues. Hues that are next to each other have an easier relationship than those that are opposite each other, which results in active complementary contrast. The concept of the advancing and receding natures of colors must also be considered. Warm colors always advance and seem nearer, while cool ones recede and seem more distant. Designers can achieve an optical fluttering of the edges of the colors in their layouts, creating an impression of lively movement. Alternatively, they can make transitions nearly invisible and ease the flow of the eye by using more harmoniously related colors. Juxtapositions of colors cause interactions, enhancing or distracting from the intended message. Proximity literally changes the character of a color. All of these context-related aspects of color can be utilized to either the advantage or the detriment of a design. Success is a matter of the intent of the piece and the skill of the designer.

Environmental Influences Change Color Perception

The end use of the piece—its particular medium— must be considered as well. A design for a retail environment involves different considerations than a design for television broadcast, for example. Both applications require that the design be seen, be understood, and communicate a given message. However, the color considerations may be totally different. A retail product package color is probably chosen in relation to other products—if every other competitor is pink and purple, then perhaps orange is a better choice. The color helps the product stand out. This is an example of the context influencing the concept as well as creating an idea that is context specific.

Lambeth First

Lambeth First is a partnership of community groups in the Lambeth area of south London. Different color combinations used for the logo represent a variety of voices, allowing color to express a multicultural context. **Atelier Works**

An illustration of color effects—how one color impacts another. Notice how the same yellow and blues look very different on the various background colors. Some combinations vibrate, some are soothing. Although the colors are used in equal amounts, some combinations make the middle squares look larger or smaller. Colors can be completely altered in expression by different juxtapositions or different contexts.

The Science of Color Comparison
Several German scientists and artists have noticed, researched, and written about the laws of chromatic contrast as well as the active role of the brain in the development of color relationships and perceptions.

Johann von Wolfgang Goethe greatly advanced color research. He was one of the first to draw attention to and describe the phenomena that can accompany colors in contrast to one another. He is most famous, however, for his approach to the treatment of color. He argued that light, shade, and hue are associated with emotional experience. His unorthodox theories of the character of light and color influenced abstract painters such as Wassily Kandinsky and Piet Mondrian.

Another influential thinker about color interaction was German physicist and meteorologist Johann Friedrich Wilhelm von Bezold (1837–1907). His professional expertise was the physics of the atmosphere, especially electrical storms, but his contribution to color physics came from his hobby—rug making. Bezold's uncle, Gustav, was a prominent art historian, which also may have influenced his foray into color research.

Light affects color

Color is light, but light also affects color. Whether it is the depiction of a real-world scene in a color illustration or the calculation of how a colored graphic may appear in its actual usage location, illumination is a factor that the designer must understand.

To create the illusion of depth in a particular piece, a designer may wish to show shadows when one form overlaps another. Whether cast by single or multiple light sources, shadows are commonly approximated by creating a shape that includes some of the complement of the original color. Also, warm light tends to cast a cold shadow, and vice versa.

Another aspect of color and light is color constancy—the tendency in human perception that allows us to compensate for various conditions and types of illumination. Color constancy is a psychophysical response that lets us recognize colors, and therefore objects, no matter what the light is like—whether it is low or bright, fluorescent, natural, or incandescent. We see an object as a certain hue because it reflects more of a particular wavelength of a specific color of light—so a tangerine looks orange because it reflects more orange light than other objects near it. Further, due to color constancy, that tangerine will seem orange to us in bright sunlight or by candlelight in a darkened room because our visual system compensates for changing illumination.

Chromatic adaptation allows for changes in environments as well. This is demonstrated when a person walks from full sunlight into a building. At first, the environment seems very dark, then our eyes gradually adapt, and true colors become apparent. Our eyes and brains are constantly adjusting to varying light conditions.

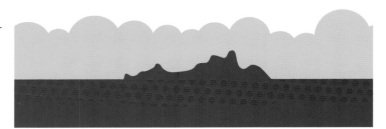

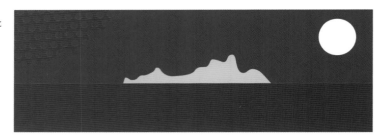

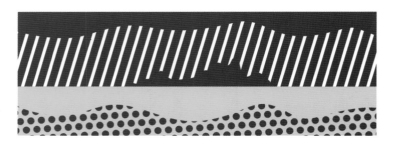

▲ A series of three full-page illustrations that accompany a *Raket* magazine article on the human fascination with islands. Nonrepresentational colors are used, stepping away from a natural color scheme. Color is used to create an abstraction of the idea of islands. The series shows that varying the color palettes in this context causes changes in the reading of images that are structurally similar.
Sweden Graphics

Bezold noticed that certain strong colors, when evenly distributed, entirely changed the effect of his rug designs. This effect is now known as the Bezold Effect. He is also known for the Bezold–Brücke Phenomenon, which is the changing perception of colors under the effects of increased light intensity; in other words, the apparent brightness of hues changes as illumination changes. His 1874 book *Die Farbenlehre in Hinblick auf Kunst und Kunstgewerbe* (*Color Theory with a View Toward Fine and Commercial Arts*) documents these findings. His work influenced Josef Albers.

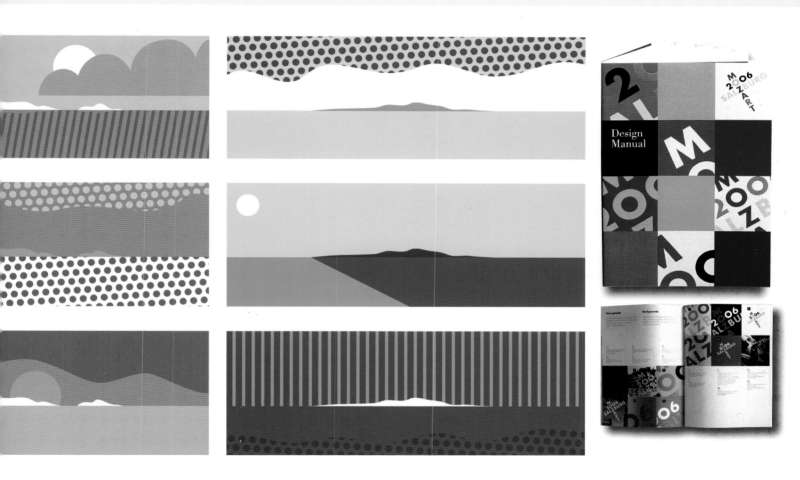

Justus Oehler designed a visual system for the 2006 cultural festival celebrating the 250th birthday of composer Wolfgang Amadeus Mozart in Salzburg, Austria. Oehler's visual system is based on a series of diagonal typographic blocks. This piece demonstrates the principle of optical mixing, in which the position of colors next to each other affect the appearance of each color. The effect can be seen here in the identity manual. The juxtaposition of these color blocks gives the illusion of even more colors and creates a lively design.
Pentagram

Simultaneous Contrast

One of the important early studies of the science of color harmony was done by French chemist Michel Eugène Chevreul (1786–1889). Chevreul introduced a systematic approach to seeing colors in his 1839 *De la loi du contraste simultané des couleurs et de l'assortiment des objets colorés* (published in English as *The Principles of Harmony and Contrast of Colors*). The book is both historically and aesthetically significant.

Chevreul was appointed the director of dyeing at the Manufacture Royale des Gobelins (the Gobelins Royal Tapestry Works) in 1824. He came to realize that many of the problems encountered in the firm's weaving had to do with how and which colors affected each other. His findings, set forth in his book, deal with simultaneous contrast.

Simultaneous contrast is a form of color mixing referred to as *medial*. This color mixing is how our eyes and brains combine colors that are next to each other to form a particular color impression. Chevreul's work on the physics of color and color effects had a great impact on the world of art. Particularly affected were the Neoimpressionists, especially the Pointillist painters Georges Seurat and Paul Signac.

In a busy, cluttered context, such as the ITC Telecom World Trade Show in Geneva, the HP Telecom booth stands out. Colors from the new HP palette were used to delineate content areas within the booth. As it was the first trade show to showcase HP's new look and feel, the color scheme served a dual purpose: as navigation to help visitors find the areas and topics they were interested in, and as a way to bring the corporate colors to life in three dimensions, signaling the emergence of the new HP brand.
Stone Yamashita Partners

The Relativity of Color

Josef Albers was a German artist and educator. He was one of the original teachers in the Bauhaus who immigrated to the U.S. and was responsible for major innovations in art education. As an artist, Albers is best known for his series of abstract paintings *Homage to a Square*; as a color theorist, he is known for his book *Interaction of Color*, published in 1963.

Albers's work demonstrates that "a color has many faces." He explored the subtle relationships among colors, and his methods of studying and teaching allow artists and designers to discover these relationships for themselves through a series of practical exercises. Among the principles Albers sought to illustrate are positive and reversed grounds (what happens when the colors of the feature elements and the backgrounds are exchanged), transparency effects (see page 47), spatial relationships (how to create the optical illusion of depth), vibrating and vanishing boundaries (see page 76), and proportional variances (see page 77). In addition, he demonstrated how all of these affect art and design.

In *Interaction of Color,* Albers takes the reader through a series of experiments, such as the one illustrated below, right, that lead to knowledge and understanding of color relationships. These exercises, too numerous and in-depth to explore here, can be used by designers to teach themselves more about color in a hands-on manner, and we recommend doing so. The Albers course, often taught in design schools, helps designers recognize and develop their own inclinations and aptitude with color.

Context became inspiration for the identity for Slade Gardens, a community adventure playground. Experiencing the park, designer Ian Childers noticed his children, dressed in bright red clothing, enjoying the elaborate green play structures. This observation resulted in the logo and its signage application.
Atelier Works

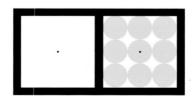

One of Albers' many experiments to show the illusion of double or reversed afterimaging, often called contrast reversal, is illustrated here. Look at the yellow circles, at left, for a minute. Now shift your eyes quickly to the lefthand square. You might expect to see the complement of yellow. However, yellow diamond shapes, mirroring the negative space between the circles, appear instead.
Josef Albers

5 Consider That Experimentation Is Key

Experimenting with color is a way of challenging a designer's imagination and often results in a variety of unexpected new solutions. Whether through changing contrast, volume, and proportion; stretching conventional notions of color harmony; or altering color temperature; new dynamics of color interaction are always possible.

Allowing one color to dominate, in contrast to others, focuses attention on design elements in that color and allows them to communicate a distinct message. Layouts that feature strong contrasts between colors in terms of hue, saturation, and value have the greatest possibilities for expressive effect. However, designers must work to unify the contrasting elements without destroying the strength and impact of the piece.

Adjusting volume or proportion—that is, experimenting with the amounts of each color used can provide interesting results. For example, a small—dark spot of color, because it is of lower value, can dominate a large light area. Also, a small amount of a warm color can dominate a larger area of a cool color, although both may have the same intensity. Proportion can be used to make a design appear light by incorporating a large area of a light hue. Conversely, large amounts of dark values make the design appear dark, even somber. Alternating color based on saturation rather than proportion completely changes the perceived visual mix of color.

Designers can use color, in either free-form or text-based layouts, as they do other graphic elements. Experimenting with colors allows designers to develop keen observations about color interactions.

"Why do two colors, put next to each other, sing? Can we really explain this? No." —Pablo Picasso

The show packaging for MTV's spring break programming features the concept of bringing bathing suit patterns to life. Creative director Todd St. John changes color palettes and gender reference to provide different interpretations of spring. Experimenting with the animation of line, proportion, and color creates variations on a theme. These variations allow for nuances in the concept yet create a strong cohesive package of promos.
Hunter Gatherer

This chart illustrates two types of dominance. *Contrast dominance,* seen in the vertical series of squares on the left, shows that contrast increases with levels of intensity or saturation. On the right, *value dominance* is shown in three compositions: first, all tints; then pure hues; and, finally, all shades.

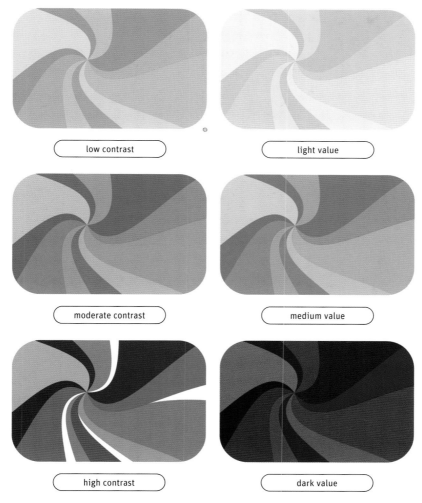

low contrast

light value

moderate contrast

medium value

high contrast

dark value

Ideas for Experimentation

There are many approaches to the idea of experimenting with color. Sometimes looking at the process from a slightly new perspective can add life and freshness to a designer's work. Here are things to consider:

- Use a restricted palette; impose your own limits on the range of colors.
- Try using colors you dislike to see if you can make a pleasing arrangement.
- Use only your favorite colors.
- Deliberately aim for concord or, alternatively, for discord.
- Choose pairs of contrasting colors.
- Subordinate your own choice of colors and work only with the client's preferences.
- Vary the scale of color usage. Allow for dominance.
- Design by choosing a mood for the piece first.
- Choose colors before shapes.
- Alter the rhythm and flow of your colors to see what happens.
- Always echo your colors. Repetition causes harmony.
- Look to the masters of fine arts, such as your favorite painter, and utilize their palettes.

Color in Professional Sports
Color has always been used to represent affiliations and loyalties, and, as such, plays a big part in professional sports.

Colors are chosen by sports teams and approved by their respective leagues. Designers and marketing experts often weigh in on the decision as well because team merchandise is big business. Colors are kept simple to translate for marketing and advertising purposes. Fashion trends seem to affect choice. Most important, colors must look good in

motion when the athletes are playing. Intense colors capture the kinetic energy of sport. In theory, team colors add a psychological edge to the team's performance. According to a Cornell University study analyzing the penalty records of twenty-eight National Football League teams from 1970 to 1986, four teams wearing black uniforms were among the

The Power of Contrast
Exploring the notion of contrast is an effective experimentation tool. Contrast is the perceived difference between adjacent colors in a design. The highest levels of contrast appear between the achromatic colors—black and white. Complementary colors also have high chromatic contrast. Contrast levels allow for aesthetic expression and determine legibility.

The famed color theorist Johannes Itten observed the following seven types of contrast:
1. **The contrast of hue:** the juxtaposition of colors at their most intense.
2. **Light-dark contrast:** formed by juxtaposition of light and dark values, including those in monochromatic compositions.
3. **Cold-warm contrast:** juxtaposition of hues that are considered warm (red, orange, yellow) or cool (violet, blue, green). Three-dimensional depth is easy to achieve with this type of contrast because of the advancing (warm) and receding (cool) characteristics of the colors.
4. **Complementary contrast:** the juxtaposition of hues opposite each other on the color wheel.
5. **Simultaneous contrast:** the contrast formed when adjacent hue boundaries perceptually vibrate as they optically mix.
6. **The contrast of saturation:** the juxtaposition of more and less saturated colors.
7. **The contrast of extension, also called the contrast of proportion:** formed by assigning proportional field sizes in relation to the visual weight of a hue.

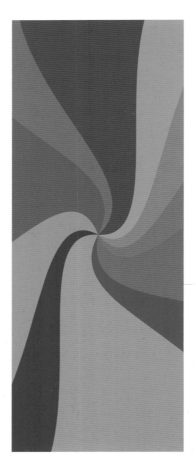

1

2

3

most penalized. Similarly, the three most penalized National Hockey League teams during that same time period wore black. These findings indicate that black may be the color associated with the most aggressive sports teams.
Our informal look at U.S. professional sports teams finds that the top four colors in order of frequency of use are:

Basketball: blue, red, yellow/gold, and black; Football: blue, black, red, and yellow/gold; Baseball: blue, red, and black, with yellow/gold a distant fourth; and Hockey: blue and red, with black and yellow/gold tied for third. Interestingly, the colors for each sport are the same, but the order of frequency differs.

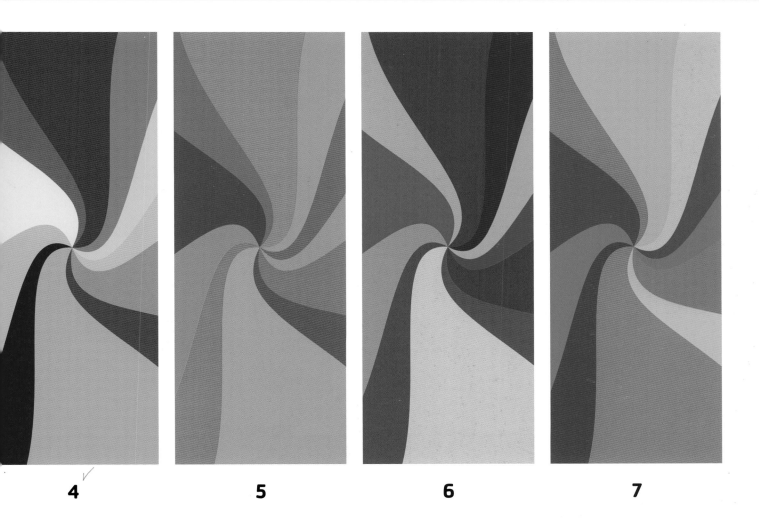

4   **5**   **6**   **7**

▲ Different types of contrast provide a variety of experiments in color relationships. All of these can be used as springboards for new ideas about colors in designs.

"Color is a means of exerting a direct influence on the soul."—Wassily Kandinsky

If/Then   0.1   1999   Dfl 69

design implications   play   Netherlands   US $29.95
of new media   Design Institute

IF/THEN   PLAY

Doors of Perception 5   digital babies   internet kiosks   board games
knowledge maps   two-ball soccer   smart cards   edible Godzillas
data butlers   elders online   bricks with brains   toys vs tools

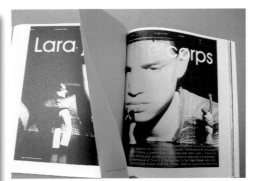

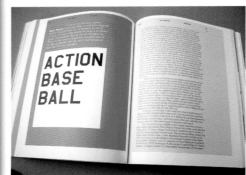

▲ The *IF/THEN* book about digital technology was designed to incorporate a sense of discovery and play. A variety of large-format black-and-white images are contrasted with rich color fields that are supplied by the insertion of different-colored paper stocks or printed as large areas of solid color. Display type in large point sizes contrasts with pages of smaller book type. Experimentation with scale, contrast, and color humanizes the high-tech subject of the book and allows access to the material.
Mevis & Van Deursen

▲ *Long Beach Architecture: The Unexpected Metropolis* incorporates an interesting and unusual use of color. Transparent color blocks are superimposed on black-and-white architectural imagery. Often, the blocks are subtle gradients of near-complementary colors. This use of color enlivens the industrial nature of the photography and creates an almost surreal posterization. True to the name of the book, the design offers an unexpected presentation of the urban landscape.
Michael Worthington

6   Know That People See Color Differently

Color vision is a result of the way our eyes and brains interpret the complexities of reflected light. What we see is a result of different wavelengths of light stimulating parts of the brain's visual system. The three types of light receptors, called *cones,* are located in the retina of the eye and recognize these different wavelengths of light. Not every human being's receptors and interpretations of color are quite the same. In addition, some people have inherited genetic conditions, such as color blindness, that further affect color perception.

Color Blindness Limits More Males

Color blindness, of which several varieties exist, affects more males than females. People with monochromatic color blindness lack all cone receptors in their eyes and cannot see any color. People with dichromatic color blindness lack either red-green or blue-yellow receptors and cannot see hues in these respective ranges. People with color weakness, or anomalous trichromatism, can perceive a color but need greater intensity of the associated wavelength in order to see it normally. The natural aging process in humans may also reduce color vision and acuity.

Physical factors are one way that people see color differently. Another factor is technological. Color is read differently in print and on the screen. Pure RGB light appears different than reflected light (usually CMYK). Colors may also appear different because not every computer monitor and television screen is color-corrected and calibrated properly. Designers cannot be sure how their color choices are being experienced in these media.

Color Alterations for Artistic Reasons

Designers may alter color perception deliberately for artistic and semiotic reasons. They may choose to subjectively or artistically change what would be considered the accurate, normal, or natural color of things, and instead render it in a different color. When a color is the real and actual expected hue, it is called a local color. If it is unexpected or abnormal, it is referred to as occult color. For example, a piece in which an apple is rendered in shades of blue would be an occult representation. A blue apple would cause the viewer to question why this familiar object is depicted in a strange and unnatural color and perhaps prompt deeper interaction with the design. This color alteration is essentially a creative interpretation or abstraction of the idea of seeing color. So when we say that people see color differently, there are a variety of issues that need consideration when designing.

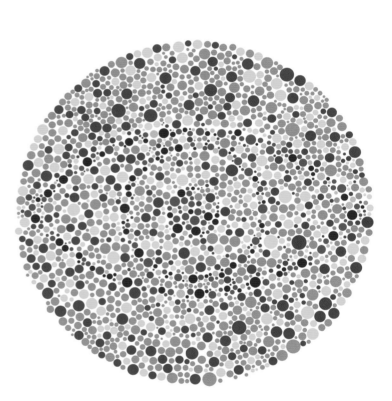

This simulation of a color blindness test graphic is like those used to diagnose red-green difficulties. People with this type of color vision deficiency cannot see the eye shape within the pattern. Several diagnostic tests are used in determining color blindness.

An Artistic Interpretation of Color

Dutch painter Vincent van Gogh (1853–1890) made a significant contribution to art through his astonishing use of color. Van Gogh used colors deliberately to capture mood and emotion rather than create realistic reproductions.

Technological advances in the chemistry of artists' pigments in the late 1800s, along with his own exposure to other Impressionists' work, freed van Gogh to use bright, intense color in his work. His palettes expanded, taking on the characteristics that made him famous.

Van Gogh painted rapidly, often using paint straight from the tube in thick impasto brushstrokes. His imaginative, vibrating, urgent color schemes changed the direction of art. He is one of the great fine art masters whose work can inspire designers.

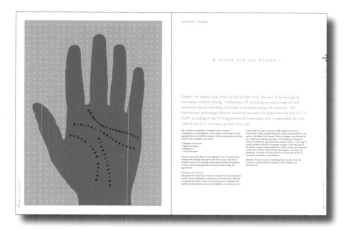

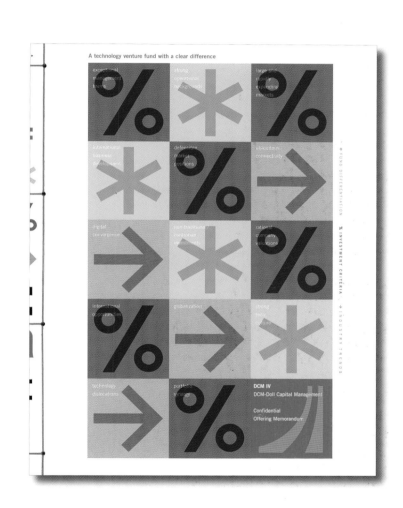

DCM (Doll Capital Management) sought to highlight the clear difference that makes its technology venture fund attractive to Asian investors. Bold graphics utilizing financial icons give an elegant simplicity to the presentation. Red was chosen as the dominant color because of its symbolic connection to luck in Asia. However, the similar tonal values in some of the monochromatic icon illustrations could be difficult for some vision-impaired people to fully appreciate.
Gee + Chung Design

Effective Color Contrast
Designing for People with Partial Sight and Color Deficiencies by Aries Arditi, Ph.D

Dr. Aries Arditi is Senior Fellow in Vision Science at Lighthouse International. The following information is based on his earlier work with Kenneth Knoblauch. It is reprinted here by permission of the author.

These are the three basic guidelines for making effective color choices that work for nearly everyone. Following the guidelines are explanations of the three perceptual attributes of color—hue, lightness, and saturation— as they are used by vision scientists.

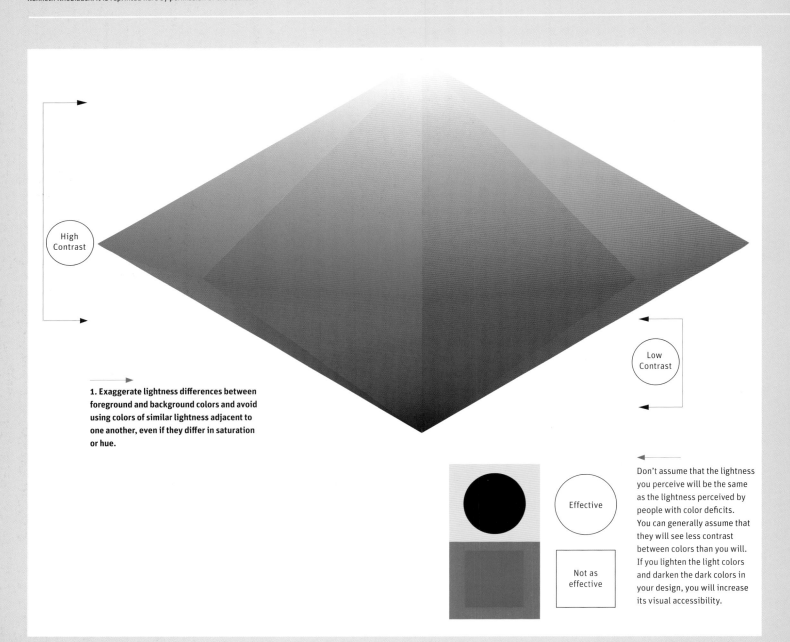

High Contrast

Low Contrast

1. Exaggerate lightness differences between foreground and background colors and avoid using colors of similar lightness adjacent to one another, even if they differ in saturation or hue.

Effective

Not as effective

Don't assume that the lightness you perceive will be the same as the lightness perceived by people with color deficits. You can generally assume that they will see less contrast between colors than you will. If you lighten the light colors and darken the dark colors in your design, you will increase its visual accessibility.

How does impaired vision affect color perception?

Partial sight, aging, and congenital color deficits all produce changes in perception that reduce the visual effectiveness of certain color combinations. Two colors that contrast sharply to someone with normal vision may be far less distinguishable to someone with a visual disorder. It is important to appreciate that the contrast of colors, one against another, that makes them more or less discernible, rather than the individual colors themselves. Here are three simple rules for making effective color choices:

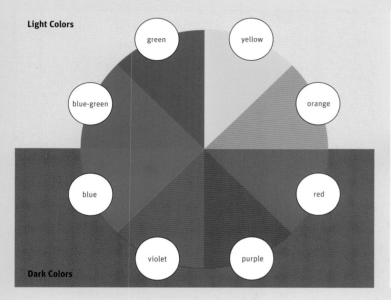

Light Colors
green yellow
blue-green orange
blue red
violet purple
Dark Colors

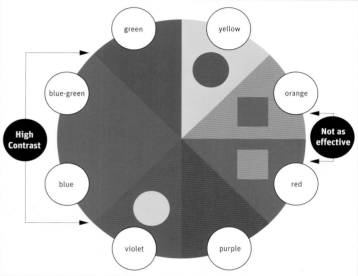

green yellow
blue-green orange
High Contrast Not as effective
blue red
violet purple

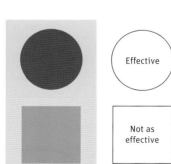

▲ **2. Choose dark colors with hues from the bottom half of this hue circle against light colors from the top half of the circle. Avoid contrasting light colors from the bottom half against dark colors from the top half. The orientation of this hue circle was chosen to illustrate this point.**

Effective

Not as effective

◄ For most people with partial sight and/or congenital color deficiencies, the lightness values of colors in the bottom half of the hue circle tend to be reduced.

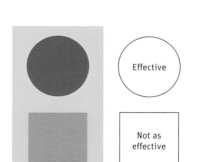

▲ **3. Avoid contrasting hues from adjacent parts of the hue circle, especially if the colors do not contrast sharply in lightness.**

Effective

Not as effective

◄ Color deficiencies associated with partial sight and congenital deficiencies make it difficult to discriminate between colors of similar hue.

"It is the contrast of colors, one against another, that makes them more or less discernible, rather than the individual colors themselves."
—Aries Arditi, Ph. D

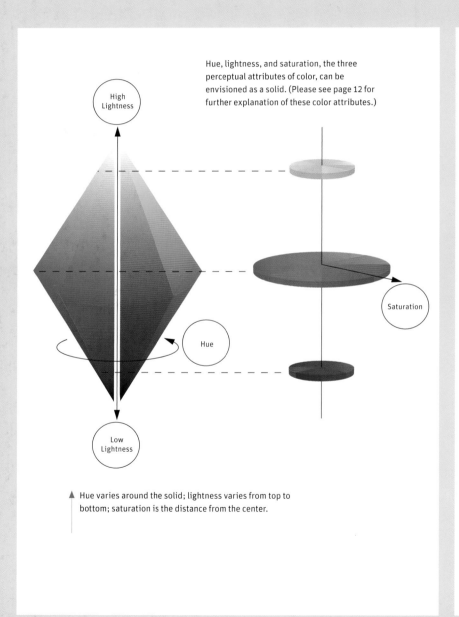

Hue, lightness, and saturation, the three perceptual attributes of color, can be envisioned as a solid. (Please see page 12 for further explanation of these color attributes.)

▲ Hue varies around the solid; lightness varies from top to bottom; saturation is the distance from the center.

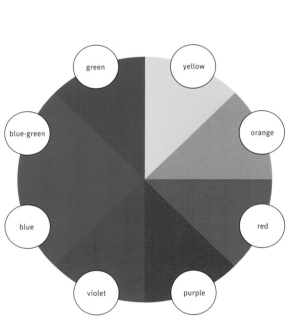

▲ Hue is the perceptual attribute associated with elementary color names. Hue enables us to identify basic color categories such as blue, green, yellow, red, and purple. People with normal color vision report that hues follow a natural sequence based on their similarity to one another. With most color deficits, the ability to discriminate between colors on the basis of hue is diminished.

About Lighthouse International

Founded in 1905 and headquartered in New York, the nonprofit organization Lighthouse International is a leading worldwide resource on vision impairment and vision rehabilitation. Through its pioneering work in vision rehabilitation services, education, research, prevention, and advocacy, Lighthouse International enables people of all ages who are blind or partially sighted to lead independent and productive lives. The Arlene Gordon Research Institute of Lighthouse International works to expand knowledge in vision impairment and rehabilitation. Dr. Aries Arditi, a senior fellow for the Institute, has written several books and brochures of use to designers on computers, typography, color, and signage. The website is www.lighthouse.org.

▲ Lightness corresponds to how much light appears to be reflected from a colored surface in relation to nearby surfaces. Lightness, like hue, is a perceptual attribute that cannot be computed from physical measurements alone. It is the most important attribute in making contrast more effective. With color deficits, the ability to discriminate colors on the basis of lightness is reduced.

▲ Saturation is the degree of color intensity associated with a color's perceptual difference from a white, black, or gray of equal lightness. Slate blue is an example of a desaturated color because it is similar to gray. A deep blue, even if it has the same lightness as slate blue, has greater saturation. Congenital and acquired color deficits typically make it difficult to discriminate between colors on the basis of saturation.

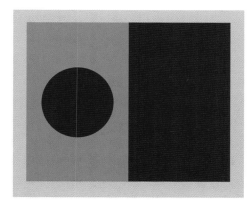

◄

To a person with color-deficient partial sight, the left-hand panel might appear like the right-hand panel appears to a person with normal color vision. With color deficits, the ability to discriminate colors on the basis of all three attributes—hue, lightness, and saturation—is reduced. Designers can help compensate for these deficits by making colors differ more dramatically in all three attributes.

(7) Assist in Mnemonic Value

What designer doesn't want his or her work to be memorable to the audiences for which it was created? Color can be a powerful ally in that pursuit. Color can work as a mnemonic device itself, aiding people's memories. The word *mnemonic* comes from the Greek *mnemonikos*, which means "mind."

Many psychologists researching the process by which humans see and process visual information conclude that it is influenced highly by color. For example, the May 2002 *Journal of Experiential Psychology: Learning, Memory, and Cognition* reported the findings of one study that indicated that people did not remember falsely colored photographic scenes any better than those same scenes in black-and-white. They remembered the natural-colored images the best. Relating to psychology, it also seems that when people think of a certain color, their minds form a corresponding color model; when they think pink, they actually visualize a rosy hue.

Color Associations Aid Memory

Different cultures have different associations with colors. Hues such as red and blue are not just colors; they are emotions, feelings, reflections, and memories. Seeing or thinking about color produces certain reactions in people. Color associations often become part of the semantic structure of color names themselves. For example, magenta, one of the first aniline dyes, was discovered shortly after the Battle of Magenta, which occurred near the northern Italian town of Magenta. The color was named for the battle and, therefore, indirectly for the town. Chartreuse is a yellow-green color named for the famous French liqueur of the same name. These types of associations are endless and can be leveraged to associate clients' products and services with colors.

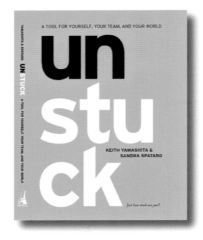

All three of these book designs utilize color in mnemonic ways. Yellow-orange is used on the cover to signal that *Unstuck* is a departure from a traditional business information book, making it memorable. In the United States, green is associated with money, making it a perfect dominant color for a book called *Naked Economics*. *Yellow in London* eschews the traditional British national colors of red, white, and blue to mirror a foreigner's unconventional perspective on the city. It is memorable because it is unexpected.

Unstuck,
Stone Yamashita Partners

Naked Economics,
Powell

Yellow in London,
Usine de Boutons

Color is memorable. Marketing research indicates that more than 80 percent of visual information is related to color.

Color Symbolism Is Culturally Linked

Interestingly, the world seems divided into groups with similar ideas about color symbolism. In a 1999 study published by Kawade Shoboh Shinsha, a Japanese professor named Hideaki Chijiiwa grouped countries as follows: China, Taiwan, and Russia; Japan, Korea, and Finland; the Netherlands, Germany, Italy, the United States, Canada, New Zealand, Australia, and Singapore; France, Brazil, and Portugal; and India, Laos, and Bangladesh. Cultural factors are at work here, and understanding the similarities and differences in audiences will always make for better design in our increasingly global community. (For a look at color associations, see the Color Index in Chapter 3.)

Cultural, political, and linguistic factors, including both abstract and symbolic components, affect our perception of colors. Color motivates a response because of memories. A person may buy the green-colored soap packaging because it reminds him or her of fresh-mown grass, for example. Couple visual information with the expected fragrance—green soap that actually smells like grass—and the design is even more effective.

Proprietary Color

A further enhancement is the idea of developing a proprietary color that represents a client. Associating distinctive colors with products and services is one of the cornerstones of brand identity work. Some of the world's most memorable companies have strong connections to color—think of Kodak's chrome yellow and Fuji's bright green film boxes. Whether or not it is possible to trademark a color is an ongoing battle, generating many lawsuits, but color is undisputedly an important branding tool.

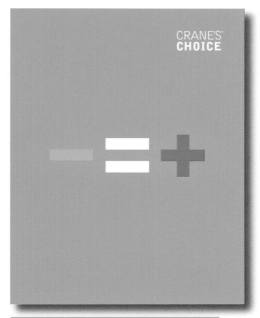

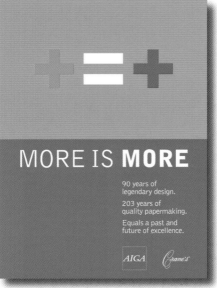

Both the − = + (Less Equals More) and the +=+ (More Equals More) promotions for Crane & Co.'s fine paper features a near-complementary color palette. The Kiehl's Education Resource Binders are an achromatic black and white color scheme. Both of these pieces are memorable because of their elegant simplicity and bold color choices.
**Chermayeff & Geismar for Crane & Co.
Liska & Associates for Kiehl's**

"Dude, Where's My Car?"

by Victoria Lam

These are spreads from a book entitled *Dude, Where's My Car?* This book represented an explorative study on how to make parking structures more memorable. The typical parking structure is bare and monotonous. As a result, users tend to erase the experience from their mind, hence the tendency to forget the location of one's car. I wanted to take this banal subject and place and propose something new as a way to intervene in the cyclical, repetitive nature of the everyday. One way in which I explored this was through the use of color. Rather than use color in a standardized way, I tried to link it to associations. For instance, if a user parked on the red floor, on the wall would be objects associated or identified with the color red. I conducted memory studies, specifically evaluating mnemonic devices, and understood that the mind thinks better in pictures. Thus, I tried to utilize an existing standard within parking structures (in this case, color) but to expand it in a way that was more functional as well as more aesthetic.

If a user were parked on the green floor, how could green be employed to transform the drab environment into something more aesthetically pleasing? What if different shades of the same color decorated the spaces on the ground? What if colored lighting enhanced the color of the level? What if objects associated with that color adorned the walls? In my memory research, I also learned that what resonates in the mind is what is extraordinary or unfamiliar. Representing something out of scale or in a manner the eye is not accustomed to aids in recall. I incorporated this idea into the green floor. Objects associated with the color green were represented not only out of context but out of scale.

Parking structures are often perceived as monolithic eyesores within cityscapes. I wanted my ideas to address this issue. What if the different-colored lights on each floor served to illuminate the building and create a fabric of colors that could vary in intensity depending on the occupancy of each level? The grid would constantly shift in color, and it would also function to communicate to passersby how full or vacant the structure was.

In terms of the design of the book, I employed color as a navigational device. The three sections of the book (introduction, memory studies, and case studies) were noted by different color tabs that fell into the gutter of the spreads.

Overall, color was an important strategy for the subject of this book. I tried to provide an alternative to the common experience that users encounter when they park their cars. The entirety of the space can be not only more memorable but also more experiential.

Victoria Lam is a Los Angeles–based graphic designer with a BA (with honors) in modern culture and the media from Brown University and an MFA in graphic design from California Institute of the Arts.

//Instead of seeing the color red, what if you saw pictures of red in context.

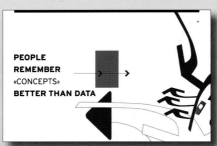

PEOPLE
REMEMBER
«CONCEPTS»
BETTER THAN DATA

THE MIND
THINKS
IN «PICTURES»

▲ Various spreads from the thesis book, *Dude, Where's My Car?* show how color might be used as a mnemonic device in parking lots and garages. Typically mundane and forgettable, parking structures could employ colorful images of red items to signify the "red floor" rather than simply marking support structures with red numbers and letters as a location device. Lam's research indicates that people actually remember color in context, such as the images seen above, even more accurately.
Victoria Lam

→ At right, schematics using colored lights in conjuction with colors painted on parking spaces themselves, this is another method of using color to aid memory.
Victoria Lam

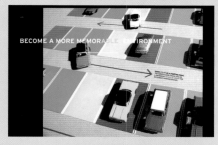

A FAMILIAR LEVEL OF A PARKING STRUCTURE CAN

BECOME A MORE MEMORABLE ENVIRONMENT

THE GREEN LEVEL COULD EXIST AMONG A GRID

OF OTHER COLORS WITHIN THE ENTIRETY OF THE STRUCTURE

THE SATURATION COULD VARY ACCORDING TO THE OCCUPANCY OF EACH SECTION WITHIN THE LEVELS

Here is an example of color graphics used in an actual garage designed by Edouard Ce-hovin. Large black, white, and red graphics positioned on the walls of a parking garage assist motorists in locating their cars and enliven the traditionally dull environment. The different-colored shapes can be used effectively as mnemonic devices.
Kontrapunkt

Color Temperature

We can identify a sensation of temperature when referring to colors—some are cool (greens, blues, violets) and some are warm (yellows, oranges, and reds). There is a contrary aspect to color temperature because color can rarely be warm and cold at once.

Warm colors are often associated with strong emotion and heat, while cool colors are linked to calmness and the refreshing chill of sky and sea. We feel color temperature— red literally makes our pulse race, while blues slows heart rates.

Considered specifically at the time of color selection, variations on and utilization of color temperature can be useful in causing designs to be more memorable and to better serve the needs of clients and their customers.

Cool Colors

Here are examples of designers working with cool colors in interesting ways. From a theater poster in Stockholm to a contract furnishings showroom environmental design to upscale dog toy packaging, cool shades of blues and greens are the unanimous choice.

Blue Skala,
Sweden Graphics

IFC Group Showroom,
Carbone Smolan Agency

For The Dogs,
Concrete

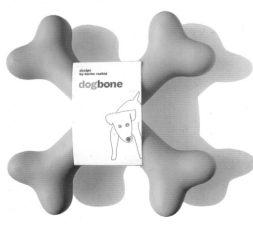

Saturation is the degree of color intensity associated with a color's perceptual difference from a white, black or gray of equal lightness. Slate blue is an example of a desaturated color because it is similar to gray. A deep blue, even if it has the same lightness as slate blue, has greater saturation. Congenital and acquired color deficits typically make it difficult to discriminate between colors on the basis of saturation.

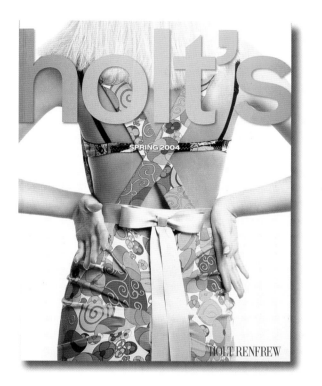

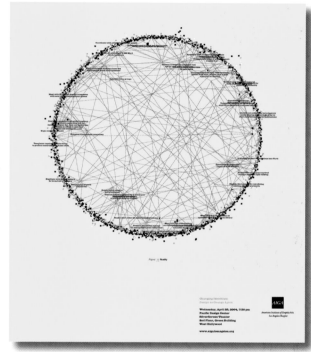

Warm Colors

Warm colors work to boost appeal in these projects, including bright earth tones for a specialty coffee store, gradient oranges for a department store catalog cover, high-impact yellow for an AIGA event poster, and melting red-orange for a television spot. Warm colors tend to advance, bringing the message to the viewer.
Holt's,
Concrete

Changing Identities
for AIGA Los Angeles,
KBDA

Terra Vida Specialty
Coffee Store,
Hornall Anderson
Design Works

Fuse,
Hunter Gatherer

8 Think About Composition

Artists have been pursuing the ideal standard for proportion and composition since ancient times. The classical Greeks established the Golden Mean, also called the Golden Section or Golden Proportion, as a mathematical ratio and unifying force. The Golden Mean is a standard proportion for width in relationship to height in which the division of a given unit of length equals the ratio of the longer part to the whole. So, if the longer part is called x, and the shorter part 1–x, then 1–x is to x as x is to 1. The Greeks understood that a small part relates to the whole, both in life and art. Other creative scholars and practitioners employ their own methods. The selection and positioning of design elements, specifically the ratio of the individual parts to one another, is a matter of the designer's personal judgment. Balance, symmetry, hierarchy, space, repetition, and rhythm are all organizing principles to be considered and used. Unquestionably, color affects all of these principles.

Color can be used to make the eye travel, comfortably or not, and pick up information from a design. Transitions can be produced using line, shape, contours (edges of shapes), and motifs in various colors for both images and typographic elements in compositions. The repetition of elements and colors create a kind of rhythm, whether a smooth flow or a jerky visual movement, as dictated by the designer's choices. The echoing of colors is a kind of repetition that brings unity to a composition. Repetition does not require exact duplication of elements; similarity, or near likeness, works. Variations in hues and their specific placement create interest, while intervals of visual silence (e.g., a dark solid-color background) between repeating elements provide rest stops for the eye. Areas of pure white and pure black boost impact and contrast.

Some designers choose to disregard traditional ideas about proportion and balance in order to emphasize extremes of scale. This creates emphasis and communicates messages through exaggeration. Differences in the scale and proportion of a color can create a focal point in a design composition.

Contour Color Study
Whether few or many colors are used, variations in composition can dramatically change a design. The four squares shown here demonstrate different proportions of color usage. Note the vibrating contours and their effect on eye movement. Also visible is the effect of vibrating and vanishing boundaries between colors.

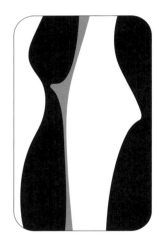
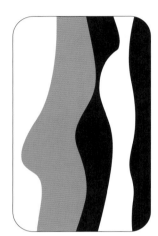
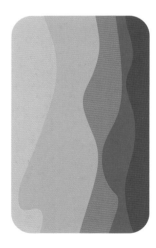

Color can be used as a visual linking device to build balanced and effective compositions.

Proportion and Saturation Study

Two pairs of color schemes—one a pair of complements, the other a triad—are shown here in differing ratios. Note how the ratio changes impact how each color is perceived and how these shifts affect the mood of the composition.

Equal proportions of the complementary colors blue and orange.

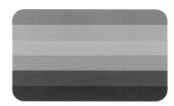

Hues of a double triad (green, red-orange, violet) used in equal proportions.

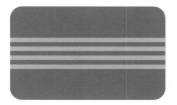

Proportions reassigned to allow dominant (blue) and subordinate (orange) areas.

Proportions reassigned to allow dominant (green), subordinate (violet), and accent (red-orange) areas.

Proportions and saturation modified, full blue on top, pure orange with a slightly desaturated blue in the middle, and desaturated blue below.

Proportions and saturation modified to display a lower level of contrast, although the central red-orange vibrates against the green areas due to their complementary relationship.

FIDM (Fashion Institute of Design & Merchandising) Museum and Galleries, under the creative direction of Tamar Rosenthal, presented the *Marimekko: Fabrics, Fashion, Architecture* exhibition to spotlight this internationally renowned design company.

The event was sponsored in part by Crate & Barrel, which created in-store displays using the exhibition poster. The composition of poster and environment reflect Marimekko's signature style.

Vrontikis Design Office

"All colors are the friends of their neighbors and the lovers of their opposites."—Marc Chagall

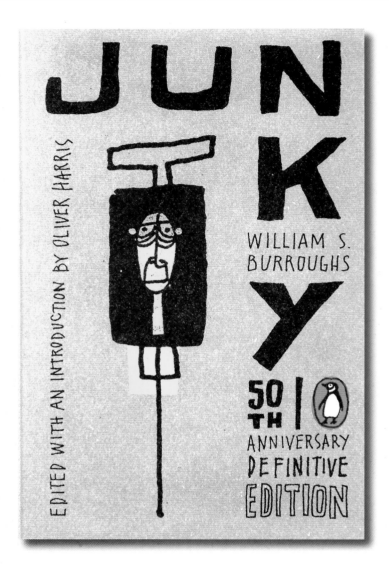

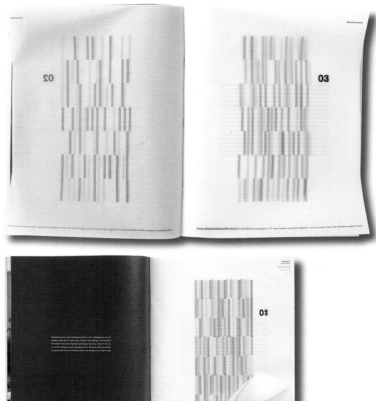

The book cover for the fiftieth anniversary definitive edition of William S. Burroughs' breakthrough novel *Junky* has a distinctive handmade quality. The composition features a hand-lettered title, a character illustration, and a hand-drawn version of the publisher's logo. The bright spots of yellow and orange leap out of the neutral background.
Powell

The Gartner Annual Report, designed by Bob Dinetz, has a graphic motif of vertical bars that repeats in several colorways throughout the book. These patterns are printed on translucent stock, allowing them to enhance and alter the typographic compositions on adjacent pages.
Cahan & Associates

The Principle of Figure and Ground

Figure and ground is an important principle in design. When we see relatively large plain elements as backgrounds to smaller, more distinct ones, we are experiencing *figure and ground*. This principle contradicts the assumption that smaller objects are always less significant—sometimes they dominate, especially due to color choice.

Compositions in which the figure and ground are not immediately distinguishable often seem lifeless and uninvolving. Elements that differ in color and value from the background draw the eye in first almost regardless of their hue. Light figures on a dark ground often seem more luminous, sometimes even mysterious—an effect exploited by Renaissance painters, for example.

The figure and ground principle, coupled with color theory ideas such as the observation that warm colors advance and cool colors recede, or that complementary colors provide rich contrast, allow a designer to create dynamic compositions.

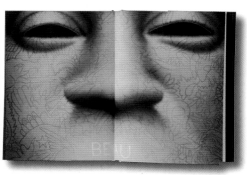

With this in a special limited-edition hardbound book, Hyatt International launched their exclusive Park Hyatt Paris-Vendôme. The book captures the grandeur and soul of the city in a series of minimally colored photographs with bold compositions, fluctuating between images with no background and images whose background make up the majority of the composition. This continually changing viewpoint brings action and life into the piece.
Louey/Rubino Design Group, Inc.

Symmetry is a distinct organizing principle in composition that can be further enhanced through the use of color.

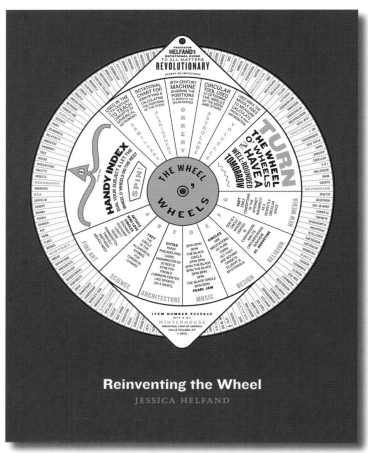

▲ **Symmetrical Balance**

Symmetrical balance is achieved by mirroring often identical elements in a composition. Symmetry can be quite static, but this *Old York* poster, commemorating the 9/11 tragedy in New York City, achieves movement through the repeating shapes of the gradient orange clouds that surround the white focal point of the Twin Towers.

Sweden Graphics

▲ **Radial Balance**

The *Reinventing the Wheel* book cover is a great example of radial balance—a composition balanced around a focal point. The designers created a volvelle, a calculation consisting of concentric circles, adapting an existing piece by retrofitting it with their own content. The complementary colors add punch to the design.

Winterhouse Editions

Closure or Visual Grouping
Early twentieth-century German gestalt psycholo-gist Max Wertheimer investigated how humans see form, pattern, shape, or total configuration in terms of group relationships rather than individual items. He discovered that several factors, such as proximity and size, help objects relate visually.

Closure, or visual grouping, is the tendency humans have to complete or unify incomplete patterns and information by bringing together the elements in their mind. Visual closure occurs when isolated elements are identified and recognized, even though a piece is missing or incomplete. Color assists in closure.

The phenomenon occurs when a designer provides minimal clues, yet the viewer brings the gestalt, or "whole effect," of closure, creating recognition and meaning in the pattern. Closure is illustrated when the halftone dots in four-color-process images pull together in a viewer's mind to create recognition. For Wertheimer, closure helped explain how artists create structural organization in their work.

▲ **Approximate Symmetry**
The poster for the film *Wolfsschlucht* demonstrates approximate symmetry, a composition in which elements that are not identical have the same apparent weight. The diagonal color blocks are not equal. The green, however, is balanced by the hue's complement in the form of a solid red figure on the right.
Format Design

▲ **Asymmetrical Balance**
Also known as *occult balance*, asymmetry is the most emotionally active form of compositional balance, as seen in this poster for an AIGA Los Angeles event about typographic evolution. Dissimilar elements, with no clear center point, are pulled together to create a pleasing off-kilter unity. Color plays a large role in the connectivity of the image, particularly with the background being a unifying gradient orange hue.
88 Phases

9 Use Standardized Color Systems

Increasingly, designers work across several media, including print, online, broadcast, packaging, and environment. Care must be given to create consistent reproduction results in a variety of manufacturing processes and materials. Consistent colors are managed through the use of standardized color systems.

Several Choices of System

For inks on paper, designers use the PANTONE® Matching System, TOYO, ANPA, or DIC (Dai Nippon Ink Colors). In the United States, the most ubiquitous color formula specification system, especially for spot colors, is PANTONE®, with colors referred to as PMS and a series of numbers (e.g., PMS185 is a bright red). These standardized colors are offered in thousands of hues as well as specialty inks such as metallics, tints, and fluorescents. Standards for soy-based ink colors are also available. Most graphic software systems (especially Adobe products), computer monitors, and ink-jet printers include palettes and simulations that correspond to these standard color systems. However, it is critical that digital devices such as monitors be properly calibrated to correctly simulate colors.

Offset lithography is a four-color process whereby layers of cyan, magenta, yellow, and black (CMYK) are applied to paper surfaces in varying amounts via dot patterns. Larger presses often include additional units to accommodate spot colors and may even have coating units to apply finishes such as varnish and aqueous coating. Standardized process color guides, which show percentages for each of the CMYK values, are available in SWOP, a printing standard used in the United States and Asia, and EURO (for Euroscale), used in Europe.

Color systems offer specification guides in a variety of formats, including binders with tear-off chips and fan-style guides. These guides also show what the colors look like on coated and uncoated paper stocks.

Greece! Rome! Monsters! is a children's book that introduces mythological stories in an innovative and engaging way. The challenge was to reproduce illustrator Calef Brown's vivid paintings in four-color process. Designer Jim Drobka incorporates hand-lettered typography that responds to the illustrations. The palette is focused on a strong and unusual purple and lime green combination that had to be accurately produced in the original English and subsequent international editions. The use of standardized color systems allowed for consistent color reproduction.
Getty Publications

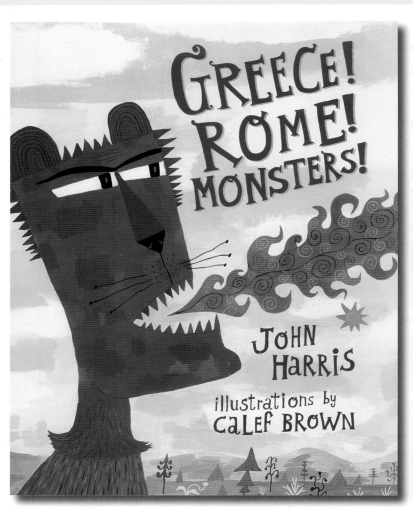

> **"We don't tend to think of paint chips as information infrastructure. Yet when everyone in the world is using the same ones, they become a communications protocol. The effect is equivalent to that of any network standard—it amplifies the scale and interconnectedness of how things get made. It greases the wheels of big, fast global culture."**
> —J. C. Herz, *Wired*, "Living Color" October 2002

Some of the latest innovations in standardized color systems are in digital color matching. For example, PANTONE® has a guide that matches spot colors with their process color equivalents and the output from several digital press systems. Guides like this ensure that a client's logo on stationery matches that in ads and brochures.

Color Standardization Beyond Print

Architects and environmental graphic designers also use a version of the PANTONE® system, as well as others, to specify textiles, paints, and plastics. Often, these must coordinate with printed components as well.

For color on screens, whether for online or broadcast, different color systems are used. To specify online colors, there are several guides for Web colors that correspond to print-based notation systems. However, graphics software, especially those for website creation, are equipped with Web-safe calibrations. For television, consistent color specification in the NTSC (in the United States) or PAL (in Europe and Asia) color space used by broadcasters is problematic. (See page 93 for further explanation of broadcast color.) The variance in preproduction, postproduction, and at-home viewing screens can be very different. There are no guides per se, but graphics software programs can convert standard CMYK colors into RGB, and good approximations of standard colors can be expected.

Color management is a complex technical issue. It is also an area that is constantly changing technologically. Designers must stay abreast of latest developments and consult with their suppliers as well as their software manufacturers' websites. They should also take advantage of the many resources and products offered by GretagMacbeth, one of the industry leaders in color management.

Posters for the HP Brand Innovation Lab's Speaker Series feature the speakers' photos rendered as monochromatic outline drawings set against a single field of one of HP's corporate colors. Spot colors like these can be consistently specified using standard color formulas.
Stone Yamashita Partners

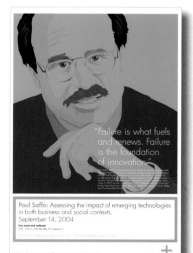

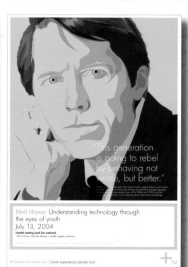

International Contract Furnishings sought to unify its collection of companies and thus established the ICF Group to provide a consolidated selling system. Marketing efforts include printer materials, advertising, online promotions, and retail stores, all designed for maximum brand coherence. That means there must be a consistent application of the corporate identity across a variety of reproduction processes and materials, as seen here.
Carbone Smolan Agency

"Color is my day-long obsession, joy, and torment."
—Claude Monet

Working with fluorescents can be tricky, but creative director David Koehler puts them to good use in the Star Financial Services Annual Report. Used as both an undercoat layer for four-color images as well as big full-bleed color blocks, fluorescents make this book stand out. Standardized guides are also available for fluorescent ink colors.
Addison Co.

These HUGA T-shirts are for sale through the designer's online store. Being able to consistently produce the same color over time is a concern for the company. Standardized specification and color formulas for silk-screening inks make this possible and can be guaranteed if the same silk-screen ink manufacturer is used for all products. Many designers use PANTONE® coated color chips when specifying color for silk- screening.
Hunter Gatherer

Color in Politics

Since the days of ancient Rome, competing political factions have used color to symbolize their group's ideologies. There are exceptions, from country to country, but the following standard associations of color and politics generally apply worldwide.

The Green Party is associated with environmentalism, and green is often used to represent Islamic parties. Blues typically represent conservative parties, except in the United States, where blue is associated with the more leftist Democratic Party. Red is historically associated with socialism or communism but now also represents the Republican Party in the United States. Both anarchism and fascism have used black, while white has been linked nearly universally to pacifism, most likely due to the white flag of surrender. Yellow is often used to represent libertarianism and liberalism. Other colors have been employed, but these are the enduring colors of politics.

The Radio Barcelona exhibition required design in several media. Color had to be managed, so standardized color systems were used to achieve consistency in items such as painted walls, printed materials, and silk-screened merchandise. Rich, deep blacks, punctuated by geometric patterns in white and pale blue, distinguish the design and give it a sense of both technology and mystery.
BASE Design

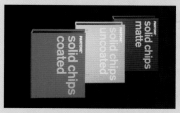

LAMENT

MUSCLE

FORTUNE

BURN

1. LAMENT

BEAUTY

OUTSKIRTS

STRIP

NOTORIOUS

Modern bodybuilding is ritual,
religion, sport, art, and science,
awash in Western chemistry
and mathematics. Defying
nature, it surpasses it.

3. FORTUNE

Instead of a single gallery guide for the
American Tableaux exhibition, eight versions
were produced, suggesting the plurality
of interpretive possibilities contained in
the theme. A new guide was available each
month during the eight-month run of the
show. All guides were then bound into a
single plastic notebook shown above right,
and at left. Color differentiates each guide,
as seen in the index, above left.
Walker Art Center

Designing for PANTONE®

Pentagram's London office had the
opportunity to design in service of standardized color systems when they worked for
PANTONE®. The firm was engaged to develop
a new identity and package design for
PANTONE® that reflected an intent to add the
general customer to the company's target
audience while retaining the existing
professional business-to-business focus.

Designers John Rushworth (Partner-
Graphics) and Daniel Weil (Partner-3D) and
their teams positioned PANTONE® to
consumers at large as the color authority
that enables them to make color-sensitive
decisions about products purchased online,
from fashion and cosmetics to lifestyle products and home furnishings. The solution
was to transform the chip icon, well known
to professional color specifiers, such as
designers, into a fun-style swatch guide.
This is a format that consumers typically
understand from buying paint and wallpaper.

Pentagram also redesigned the PANTONE®
matching system guides for designers and
printers, reaffirming their fundamental value
as unique and comprehensive technical
references while enhancing their usability.
Each manual is now color-coded by system
and held in clothbound binders to convey a
tangible sense of quality. The typographical
language suggests an accessible and ordered
authority, inspiring confidence in the
technical qualities of the brand.

(10)   Understand Limitations

It has been said that necessity is the mother of invention, and naturally, that applies to graphic design as well. Sometimes budget constraints are a limiting factor that wears down and frustrates designers. Stretching design dollars does not mean that down and dirty must be ugly and ineffective. Effective color usage can provide impact and beauty on a limited budget. Financial concerns are not the only reason for limiting the number of colors specified; sometimes it is a question of aesthetics as well.

Using only a few colors, perhaps on colored stocks, can result in a rich-looking piece. Pushing the boundaries with limited resources often means pushing the limits of production technology or thinking of new ways to incorporate old manufacturing techniques and materials. Stretching design dollars means embracing and leveraging limitations. However, it is best to understand the client's budget up front so designs can be formulated within it.

Delivery Media Affects Color
There is a vast difference between the way color works on coated versus uncoated paper stocks. It is important to design and prepare artwork correctly for the paper type being used in order for the specified colors to look their best. Uncoated stocks absorb more ink, so color tends to sink or flatten unless separations are made to compensate for this.

Halftone dots in color images tend to spread and deform on uncoated paper, a problem known as dot gain. Therefore, scanning and separations must compensate by opening the dots more so colors will appear to be at normal densities.

Coated stocks are made by casting the paper against highly polished, heated steel drums. The result is a harder surface that provides what is known as ink holdout, meaning that the color stays on the surface and is not absorbed into the paper. Both paper types have their own appeal, and colors will look great on each if the designs are properly prepared.

Color on screens—computer monitors or television sets—has its own limitations. The designers' biggest challenge is their inability to control the end product; each screen's calibrations and display properties are beyond the reach of standardized color specifications. For example, Macintosh and Windows operating systems use different platforms and protocols, and color can look very different in each.

Manufacturers work within a variety of technical parameters. Consumers can also make personal adjustments in image quality and color saturation. The result is that designers never really know whether their work is being viewed exactly as they intended it to or not.

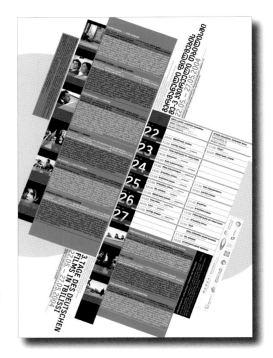

▲ This is the program for the *Tag Des Dutchmen Films in Tbilisi* film festival. Budget constraints required that it be printed with two colors, cyan and black, on the back of the event poster. The program contains a schedule, film descriptions in two languages, and still images from each movie. Transparencies, pattern, and typography all work to produce a strong visual statement seemingly unhindered by budget.
Andrea Tinnes

"Design depends largely on constraints."
—Charles Eames

Miracle Creations is a designer toy shop in Singapore that sells interesting collectibles sourced from around the world and manufactures its own unique handmade toys as well. A corporate identity package was created that incorporates a series of magical and fairy tale creatures illustrated as silhouettes. The stationery is all fit on a large A2 sheet, separated by perforations that provide the design with an interestingly interactive twist. Only Rhodamine Red (in positive and reverse color formats) was used, in order to limit costs. The red is fun and stands out against the stark white, giving the piece a surreal feel because it is an unnatural color for the imagery used.

Kinetic

Color on Paper

The key to great color on paper is working closely with your printer both in preproduction and on press. The dimension of color is always a concern, especially if you like very saturated, vibrant colors like we do at AdamsMorioka. Here are some tips for great results:

• Tell your printer up front if you'll be specifying coated or uncoated paper stock.

• Get samples of the paper. Ask for "commercial printed samples" because these are actual print jobs from designers like you, and you can see real-world results. If your printer has run this stock before, ask for these samples as well.

• Provide your printer with any production and technical information you may have from the paper manufacturer. They often have great guidelines.

• Make sure your scans and separations for uncoated stocks compensate for dot gain.

• Make sure to compensate for the color of the paper itself. For example, reduce yellows in scans of images to be used on a cream-colored stock to achieve an accurate reproduction.

• Let your printer know in advance if you'd like to use specialty inks such as soy based, metallics, or fluorescents.

• Request an "ink drawdown," which is a sample of the ink you've chosen on your actual paper stock.

• Add fluorescent ink touch plates under large areas of four-color process to add vibrancy to image color on uncoated papers. Using UV inks will also add richness to colors on uncoated stock.

• On press, make sure your printer takes both a wet and dry ink-density reading. Because uncoated stocks take longer to dry, the variances could be dramatic. Make sure the printer records this if there is a possibility of future reruns on the job.

• Preparation saves time, money, and disappointment and is the key to getting great color on paper.

How We Perceive Color over Time
Aging is a natural human limitation. Color perceptions and preferences change with a person's age.

A study in Germany conducted by anthropologist Dr. Manuela Dittmar showed that age group differences in both males and females affected color preferences significantly. With advancing age, people's preference for blue steadily decreased, while the popularity of green and red increased.

The results suggest that color preferences can change over the course of the adult lifespan. These changes might be attributed to alterations in the ability to discriminate colors, the yellowing of the crystalline lens of the eye, and the decreased functionality of the retina's blue cones.

SamataMason was the Creative Director for this Appleton Paper promotion, consisting of a series of small books created by different designers and contained in a black case. Each book interprets the same theme and utilizes the same black and red color palette. The directive of the series was to "offer meaningful thoughts and insights in a frenetic age of meaningless information and vapid graphic metaphors," as described by one of the book designers, John Bielenberg. Subjects included numerous translations of jokes, poetry, showcases, a sociological study of designers, and a personal diary. It is interesting to see the variety of graphic results using the same set of color limitations.
SamataMason, Creative Directors

"Limitations motivate creativity."
—Sean Adams

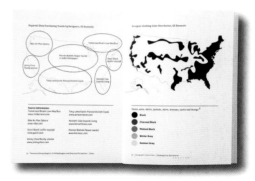

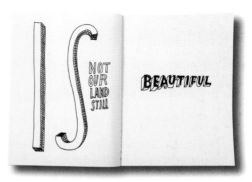

Above are the Appleton Utopia books created by AdamsMorioka, Concrete, John Bielenberg, Michael Mabry, SamataMason, Howard Belk, and Stefan Sagmeister.

Using color on screens should carry this warning:
WYSIPNWYG (What You See Is Probably Not What You'll Get).

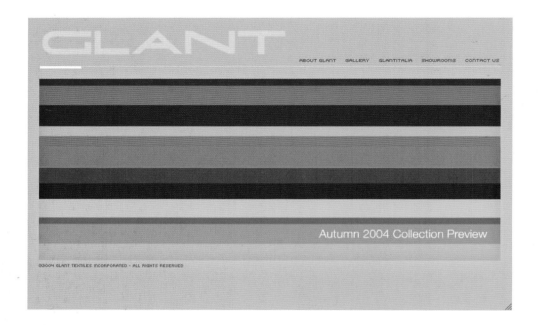

Motion Theory and Weiden + Kennedy/Tokyo collaborated to merge graffiti, an urban art form, and sophisticated motion graphics to promote Nike Presto to a Pan-Asian market. Colorful graffiti paintings literally come off the wall in animated television commercials. Graphics are intercut with Tokyo and Shanghai street scenes set to the music of Japanese DJ Uppercut, all toward the goal of capturing the spirit of art, music, and culture of contemporary Asia.
Wieden + Kennedy/Tokyo
Motion Theory

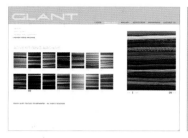

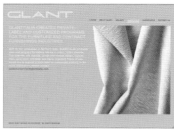

The Glant website takes advantage of the unique qualities of design for the web. Glant designs and manufactures fine textiles, primarily for use in interior design, in the United States and Europe. Built mostly in HTML, the site functions as an online catalog, so reproductions of product textures and colors are critical. The use of a neutral gray background throughout the site creates a unified feeling and allows the photos of the Glant products to stand out on screen.
Methodologie

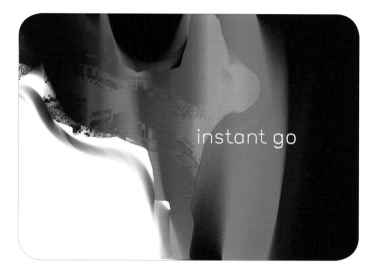

instant go

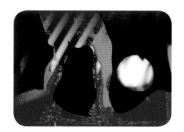

Color On Screen: Design for Web & TV
by Victor Bornia

If you are color-obsessed, bristling at anyone who mistakes your eggshell for white, you may need to ease up when it comes to designing for the screen.

Color and Web Design

Any use of color online—intended for viewing by the masses on personal computer screens—is far more of a hit-or-miss affair than color on paper. Once the design is on-line, it will be viewed on different platforms (Macintosh, Windows, etc.), each with their own gamma curves on different monitors (e.g., CRT, LCD), each set to brightness and contrast levels that no designer can control. That deep, lush burgundy you specified might be blown out to fire engine red, while that subtle pattern of darker hues you designed as a background may well end up a solid black. However, the disparities are not that ridiculous now that technology has advanced, and most people view websites in 24-bit color.

Basic Web Design Tips

- Test your design on both Macintosh and Windows computers. See the resulting variances for yourself.
- Try simulating a variety of brightness and contrast levels to see how your design stands up.
- Understand graphics formats. The basic rule is that images composed of solid colors (type, icons, etc.) should use GIF; photos or complex images should use JPEG. Try both when exporting your graphics for the Web to see what works best— that is, creates the smallest files with the best-looking result.

Color and Broadcast Design

The problem with designing for broadcast is similar to taking your design to the computer screen (which is RGB) and preparing it for print (to CMYK). However, rather than go flat or dull, colors now explode. This is because the standard television color space for video in the United States is NTSC (National Television System Committee). PAL (Phase Alteration by Line) and SECAM (Systeme Electronique Couleur avec Memoire), in Europe and Asia, all use a different gamma curve for luminance than your computer monitor. For example, any dark or muddy areas in your design may well blossom into vivid detail when viewed on an NTSC monitor.

Video also uses a different color space (YUV instead of RGB) and is often subject to limitations on what can be recorded onto a particular format (e.g., videotape). As a result, what you see on your computer monitor will only get you so far in predicting what you will see on video. Only using an NTSC monitor allows you to see what the design will really look like. The good news is that most video software allows for a simple FireWire connection to an NTSC monitor, so you can keep tabs on the results as you design (you'll need a FireWire NSTC breakout box as well). Also, most video graphics software (e.g., Adobe Aftereffects, Apple's Final Cut Pro, etc.) have a built-in shortcut—a broadcast safe filter that attempts to automate the process of making your colors ready for television.

Basic Broadcast Design Tips

- Always view your work on a properly calibrated NTSC monitor. If that is not possible, use a television with a video-in jack. It will serve as a NTSC monitor and will be more accurate than viewing on your computer monitor.
- Do not trust built-in filters exclusively to go broadcast safe. Use your own eyes; sometimes desaturating an image works best. At other times, adjustments to the brightness or contrast will be required.
- Test designs in their final delivery format. Laying off to VHS affects images differently than MPEG-2 encoding required for DVD.
- Read books by Trish and Chris Meyer, especially *Creating Motion Graphics*. They provide excellent advice.

Victor Bornia made the transition from print to Web (producer for an online music magazine) to motion graphics (led workshops in Aftereffects for Adobe) to visual effects (member of the Emmy Award–winning team in 2001 for Star Trek: Voyager*). He currently works as a 3-D animator in Los Angeles.*

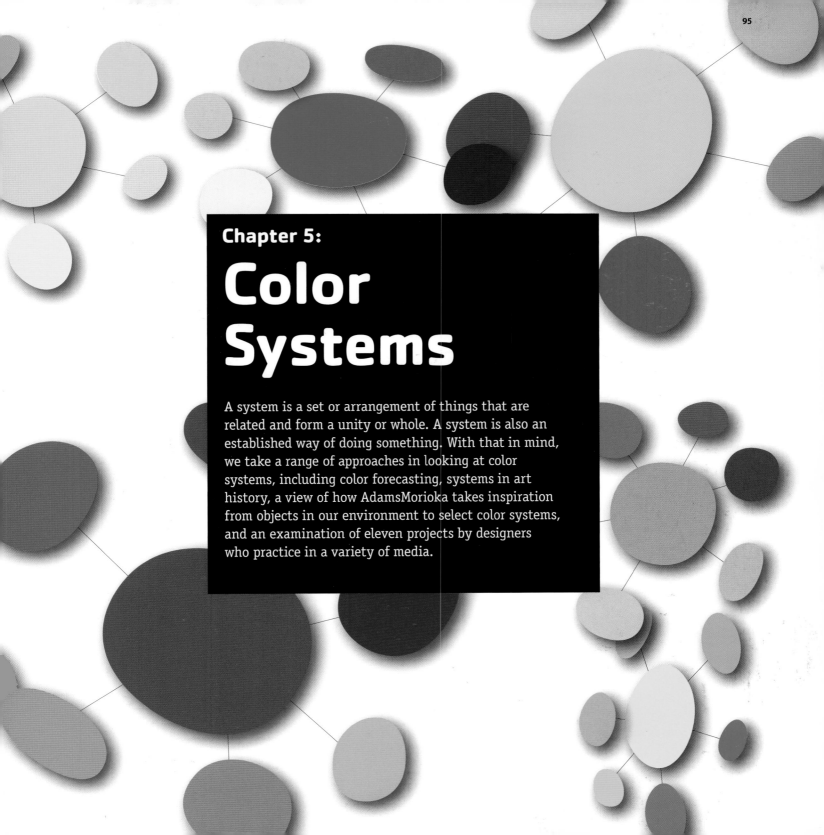

Chapter 5:
Color Systems

A system is a set or arrangement of things that are related and form a unity or whole. A system is also an established way of doing something. With that in mind, we take a range of approaches in looking at color systems, including color forecasting, systems in art history, a view of how AdamsMorioka takes inspiration from objects in our environment to select color systems, and an examination of eleven projects by designers who practice in a variety of media.

Thinking About Color Systems
Trends and Forecasting

"The forecasting business is notoriously intuitive. Forecasters work too far in advance of the market to offer the client any hard and fast data beyond their own track record."
—Rick Poynor, *Obey The Giant*

Several companies, designers, and associations do market research on color to establish trends and predict changing cultural preferences that impact all areas of design. A variety of indicators, including consumer testing and surveys, help these color forecasters issue projections and define color palette preferences they believe will rise, fall, or maintain popularity. Most design-driven industries keep these projections in mind when developing their products.

Some industries find that color trends change rapidly; others are less subject to fluctuations in taste and style. The fashion industry is perhaps the most susceptible to trend. However, interior design, especially home furnishings, and automotive design are subject to fluctuations as well. Youth-oriented goods and services in every category feel the effects of shifting color trends.

The major U.S. forecasters are the PANTONE® Color Institute, the Color Association of America (CAUS—the oldest forecasting service in the country), and the Color Marketing Group (a nonprofit international association of 1,500 color designers). These groups provide forums, workshops, and reports on an annual and seasonal basis.

Color trends are huge design variables. Color forecasting helps designers look into the future to try to understand what colors will be not only fashionable but appropriate for their projects. One way to create work that has lasting appeal is to use the rainbow spectrum colors shown in this illustration for Quattroporte by Marco Morosini.
Marco Morosini

Color Cycles
Many factors affect color trends, including:
- **National cultural influences**
- **Music and entertainment; pop culture**
- **The economy (good or bad)**
- **World events (politics, wars, natural disasters)**
- **The shrinking global community**
- **Business and manufacturing demands**
- **Nature and environmentalism**
- **Shared technologies**
- **Nostalgia and futurism**
- **Psychological impact of certain colors**

Color Forecasts: Where Do They Come From?
By Leatrice Eiseman

From international runways to America's own designer collections, the march of models in the latest trend of colors will ultimately wend its way into and greatly influence the color of interior furnishings, automobiles, and all manner of consumer goods, including product packaging, advertising, websites, and point-of-purchase appeal.

The designers themselves are the stars of the show. They are attuned to and inspired by the hues they choose for a given season: they mold and manage color so that it attracts or titillates the consumer's eye.

Obviously, fashion designers feel that color is an integral element of their work and recognize the emotional tug at the consumer level. The colors that appear first in fashion will trickle down inevitably to other design sensibilities, including graphic design.

In this modern age of instantaneous global communication, the pecking order is not as rigid as in the past, when new colors were first embraced by fashion, where they remained firmly entrenched

manufacturers adapted them for other design areas. Today the crossover of colors can happen within a matter of days as graphic designers access and adapt to the latest trends.

In the late 1980s, environmentalism was gaining ground as a sociological issue. That encouraged the use of recycled paper and discouraged the use of toxic chemical inks that were used in bolder colors. As a result, nonbleached hues such as beige and off-white became the colors of the moment in consumer goods, including clothing, home furnishings, packaging, and paper.

More recently, the graphic arts industry has spawned some of the most creative and unique color combinations and outrageous images that are constantly flashing on www.whatever.com. Colors bombard the public from a variety of other venues as well—from point-of-purchase to slick magazines, newspapers, catalogs, and billboards to the ubiquitous fashion reports on MTV, E! Entertainment Television, and CNN. As a result of all this exposure to color, the consumer is savvier than ever; he or she expects to see new color offerings in all products, so it behooves the smart designer to stay ahead of the curve.

To stay on the cutting edge of what is happening in color, it is imperative to understand the events that brought them to the forefront. From a purely psychological and sociological perspective, forecasted colors are inspired by lifestyle. For example, when designer coffee became the rage in the mid-1990s, coffee browns came forward in every area of design.

The attitudes and interests of the public at large—not only through entertainment and fashion icons and their important social concerns, needs, desires, fears, and fantasies may spawn the newest color trends.

Leatrice Eiseman, the executive director of the PANTONE Color Institute, is an internationally recognized color specialist. She is widely quoted in the media and is the author of several books, including PANTONE Guide to Communicating with Color. *For more information, visit www.colorexpert.com.*

olor Systems in Art and Design History

et's Impressionism

ressionism was a major art movement that emerged in France during the late nineteenth
twentieth centuries. Formed by a group of artists who shared related approaches and
niques, the hallmark of the style is the attempt to capture the subjective impression of light
scene. Claude Monet is the archetypal Impressionist due to his devotion to the ideals of the
ement. His famous studies *Haystacks*, *The Rouen Cathedral*, and *Waterlilies* record the subtle
sations of reflected light with the passage of time. His use of small brushstrokes of pure,
nse, unmixed hues requires the participation of the viewer, whose eyes must mix colors
approximate the experience of natural sunlight.

Couscous
book
Ph.D

thwestern Adobe

Southwestern Adobe style is based on the beautiful arts and crafts of the native peoples
e American Southwest, especially the Anasazi, Navajo, Apache, and Zuni Indians, and
sed by Spanish and Mexican cultures. While the Southwestern style has been developing for
turies, it was popularized in the 1980s, almost to the point of cliché. Warm adobe sun-dried
ks used in house construction, textiles, baskets, and turquoise and silver jewelry all express
influence this style. Age-old materials of heavy rough-hewn wood, terra-cotta tile, and
ught iron against the unmatched landscape of the high desert with its expansive plateaus,
inctive mountains, and glorious red-orange sunsets can only be found in the Southwest.

Eat
Pentagram
Design, Lt

ican Folklorica

timeless traditional Mexican folk arts and crafts combine traditions of Mesoamerican roots
inspirations with European, particularly Spanish, influences. The sacred and profane mix is
nd of Mexican baroque that incorporates native Indian decorative motifs, Catholic religious
ography, and lively narratives from everyday life. The bright, vivid colors are essential
e bold imagery, full of joy and human activity. The art and handicrafts are primarily of a
esentational figurative style, not at all abstract, and full of a simple splendor reflecting the
racter and ingenuity of Mexican artisans. There is a fluid romantic beauty and soulful rustic
quity to this sun-drenched style.

Anti-Drug
(detail)
**Brand
Integratio.
Group/
Ogilvy &
Mather**

can *Kente*

can art fuses visual aesthetics and imagery with spiritual beliefs and social purpose.
nical and artistic perfection merge in the gorgeous traditional *kente* cloth, which dates to
fth-century Ghana. These textiles were originally worn by royalty and important figures of
e for ceremonial occasions. Today *kente* cloth is often worn with pride as homage to African
tage. *Kente* comes from the word *kenten* ("basket") due to its resemblance to intricate basket
gns. Skilled artists work to create balance and symmetry in the carefully woven designs.
complex pattern of vibrant colors has deep symbolic meaning that represents the history,
osophy, ethics, and moral values in African culture.

24/7 (detai
Ph.D

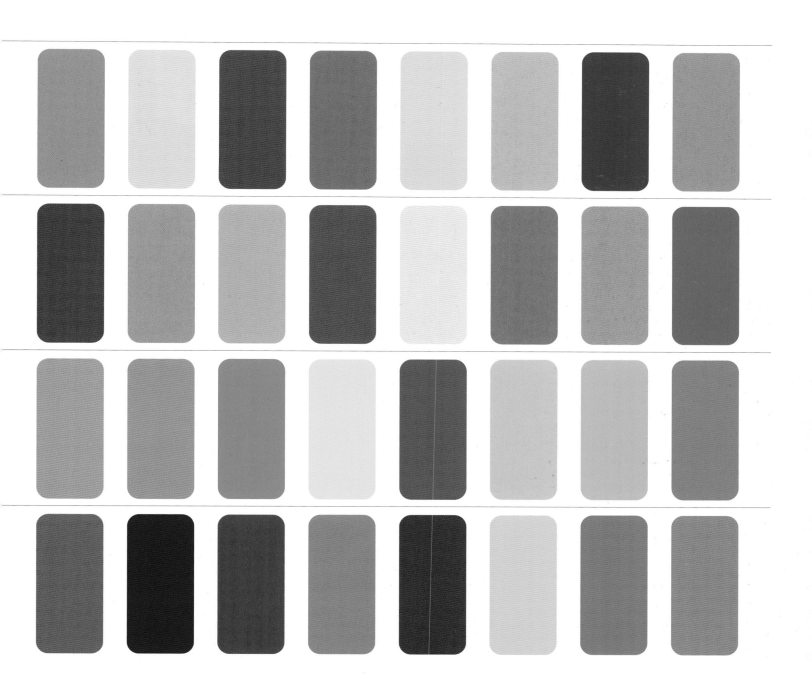

Color Systems in Art and Design History

Medieval Stained Glass

During the Gothic age, with its apex in the fifteenth century, the great cathedrals of Europe were built with spectacular pictorial stained glass windows. These luminous walls of glass were meant to lift men's souls closer to God. Stained glass is a bit of a misnomer, because most consist of colored pieces of glass held together with strips of lead. These transparent mosaics portray biblical history and church dogma. In the hands of medieval glaziers, the glass took on a jewel-like quality with the prevailing colors being red, blue, green, purple, purplish red, saffron yellow, reddish yellow, and small amounts of white. Stained glass is one of the most beautiful forms of medieval artistic expression.

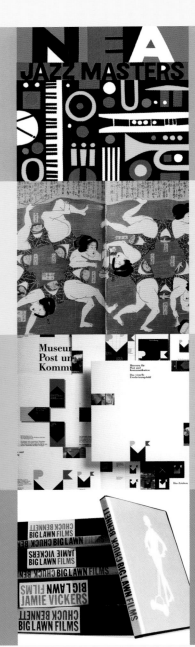

NEA Jazz Masters (detail) **Chermayeff & Geismar, Inc.**

Japanese *Ukiyo-e*

An art form both populist and sophisticated, *ukiyo-e* is the exquisite wood-block printmaking of the Edo period (1600s–1867) in Japan. *Ukiyo* translates as "floating world," an ironic wordplay on the Buddhist term for the sorrowful earthly plane. *Ukiyo* was the name given to the lifestyle of the urban centers involving fashion, the high life, and the pleasures of the flesh. *Ukiyo-e* images document both historical themes and popular culture, with an emphasis on kabuki actors, geishas, and landscapes. Early prints are spare and monochromatic. Later works are multicolored *nishiki-e* (brocade pictures) with a rich palette. These prints heavily influenced European artists, particularly French Impressionists.

View From Here book (detail) **Green Dragon Office**

de Stijl

An art movement of the early 1920s, *de Stijl* (Dutch for "the Style") advocated simplicity and pure abstraction. De Stijl artists were interested in creating a universal style, accessible to all. Their utopian philosophical approach, advocating a purification of art and austerity of expression, was demonstrated in a variety of art forms as well as a journal bearing the name of the movement. Their carefully orchestrated straight lines and flat planes were a kind of ordering of reality. The color palette of primaries and achromatic colors (white, gray, black) helped take abstraction to its purest form. Although their output was small, de Stijl artists heavily influenced many subsequent design styles.

Museum Post und Kommuni-cation **Pentagram**

Tropical Art Deco/Streamline Moderne

This style is best exemplified by the Miami Beach, Florida, oceanside district of small hotels, private residences, and commercial buildings developed in the 1930s and early 1940s. Tropical Art Deco, a later phase of Art Deco, is sometimes referred to as Streamline Moderne. This distinctive style incorporates clean modern lines and machine-inspired architectural forms of optimistic futurism mixed with local tropical imagery in the form of relief ornamentation of whimsical flora and fauna. Most remarkable is how delightfully the pale pastel color palette stands out in the bright sunlight reflecting off white sand beaches and sparkling waters.

Big Lawn Films **Ph.D**

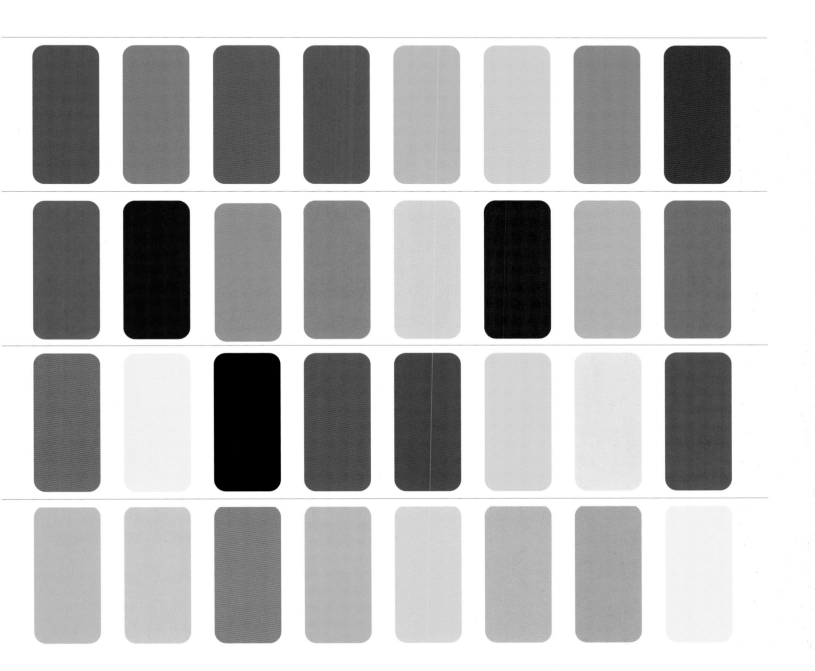

Some Inspirations for a Sample of AdamsMorioka's Palettes

Raffiaware cups

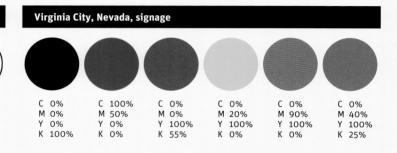

C 50%	C 50%	C 50%	C 0%	C 0%	C 0%
M 0%	M 20%	M 0%	M 20%	M 60%	M 0%
Y 20%	Y 0%	Y 100%	Y 100%	Y 80%	Y 20%
K 0%	K 0%	K 35%	K 0%	K 0%	K 0%

Virginia City, Nevada, signage

C 0%	C 100%	C 0%	C 0%	C 0%	C 0%
M 0%	M 50%	M 0%	M 20%	M 90%	M 40%
Y 0%	Y 0%	Y 100%	Y 100%	Y 100%	Y 100%
K 100%	K 0%	K 55%	K 0%	K 0%	K 25%

Interesting color schemes can be motivated by everyday objects, as well as traveling, here are a few things that have inspired us.

American desert landscape

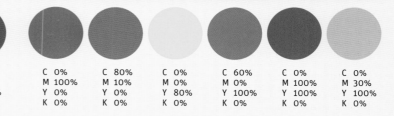

C 50%	C 50%	C 0%	C 0%	C 0%	C 20%
M 0%	M 0%	M 0%	M 25%	M 10%	M 50%
Y 35%	Y 0%	Y 100%	Y 10%	Y 20%	Y 100%
K 25%	K 25%	K 75%	K 0%	K 10%	K 20%

Asian mass-market products

C 0%	C 80%	C 0%	C 60%	C 0%	C 0%
M 100%	M 10%	M 0%	M 0%	M 100%	M 30%
Y 0%	Y 0%	Y 80%	Y 100%	Y 100%	Y 100%
K 0%	K 0%	K 0%	K 0%	K 0%	K 0%

Design Firm:

Chase Design Group

Polly Pocket! Licensed Product Style Guides Design
Client: Mattel, Inc.

Polly Pocket! is a product line centered around a small toy doll. The first job assigned to Chase Design Group was to update the personality at the heart of the brand: Polly herself. This included exploring Polly's likes and dislikes, defining her style preferences, and giving her a lifestyle and friends. Next, an entire line of graphics, patterns, and illustrations was designed, along with concepts for soft and hard line products such as apparel, electronics, and activities that would support the brand.

The goal of these licensing guides is to create a line of products that parents and their four- to eight-year-old girls will want to buy and wear. Unlike many licensing brands, Mattel's brands are built on familiar toys but are not supported by entertainment properties such as movies and television shows. Therefore, the designs themselves must work hard to make a strong fashion statement that will appeal to consumers. Chase Design Group not only created the binders, but also designed the colorful graphics to be used to create the merchandise.

▲ Produced twice a year, these guides feature predominantly lime green and red. This core palette was expanded to include orange and purple and allows for additions of seasonal colors as well.

The original Polly Pocket! illustrations lacked style and personality, so they were redrawn in a more modern, slightly anime style. The existing color palette was adjusted and expanded to be more fashion-forward and work better for apparel. A simple iconic style was developed for the art, pattern, and graphics so it can be maintained consistently throughout the product lines yet updated with seasonal changes.

Design Firm:

Durfee Regn Sandhaus

"The World from Here: Treasures of the Great Libraries of Los Angeles" Exhibition Design

Client: UCLA Hammer Museum
Curators: Cynthia Burlingham, Bruce Whiteman, Wim de Wit

The World from Here exhibition provides a rare window into the rich holdings of Los Angeles' libraries. Through the exhibition design, Durfee Regn Sandhaus (DRS) sought to create an environment that allows an intimate appreciation of books and documents, encouraging a deeper understanding of the works as objects and as important artifacts in the history of ideas.

The design creates a supportive environment for quiet reflection and enjoyment of the books featured in the exhibition. Visual activity is limited to the insides of the display cases. Special lighting conditions produce both excellent visibility for the objects and a glowing space with treasurelike moments of light.

The exhibition invites a deeper appreciation of rare books. This reading room features a wall graphic with the X motif in the refined color palette chosen.

The motif of an *X*, often seen on treasure maps in red, is used throughout the exhibition to suggest "*X* marks the spot" as well as to reflect the many "heres" referred to in the exhibition's title.

Reading rails and continuous table-height surfaces flow through the gallery, unifying the diverse elements and their display conditions.

A wall graphic schematic shows the exhibition's pale blues, grays, and golds punctuated by a deep red. The *X* points to the idea of *here*, as in Los Angeles, the library, or the book itself as a point of departure into new worlds.

Design Firm:

Hello Design

"Culture Shock Week" Website Interface Design
Client: The National Geographic Channel

The National Geographic Channel sought to promote its special weeklong programming event called "Culture Shock Week" to drive television tune-in and attract new viewers to the channel. To help promote the on-air programming, an online photography contest was developed. Users submitted their own photos from around the world, revealing both foreign cultures and diversity within the United States.

"Culture Shock Week" unveiled taboos throughout the world by looking at forbidden rites and rituals in many cultures. An online identity and visual system was created to present this unique programming in a compelling user experience. The website featured an easy-to-use interface that was templated for reuse with the "Culture Shock Week" photo gallery and future promotional sites for the client.

▲ The dominant color used is a rich dark red/maroon, chosen because it is earthy, bold, and vibrant. It resonates with the event's focus on culture, ethnology, and society. The boldness of the maroon grabs attention without being overwhelming, especially as it is balanced by black bars and the photos themselves.

▲ A simple, scrollable interface allows users to browse additional information and images in a visual way, customizing the experience to the user. Program listings and descriptions about other "Culture Shock Week" shows are provided in an area of white type on a black background. Users can quickly seek additional information on the shows and support viewership of the channel.

▲ The navigational system for the photo gallery appears as a series of vertical bars below the photo box. Thumbnail views that enlarge when selected allow users to browse as well as look at an image up close. This design encourages interaction with gallery content.

The site is bold and visually stimulating, with rich beautiful *National Geographic* photography that underscores the fascinating cultures, peoples, and rituals everywhere.

Design Firm:

Liska & Associates

**2002 Product Catalog and Dealer Toolkit
Klein Bicycles**

Klein Bicycles is a favorite of professional racers and hardcore mountain bikers, but few outside that small circle of devotees knew of the brand's existence until recently. Since 2000, Liska & Associates has helped build the Klein brand and raise awareness in an audience that purchases luxury sports equipment.

These goals are accomplished by focusing on the proprietary advantages built into a Klein bicycle's design and by positioning Klein as a best-of-class brand. Two pieces that have been key to the successful brand efforts are the catalog and the dealer toolkit. Both heavily emphasize Klein's custom paint color program options.

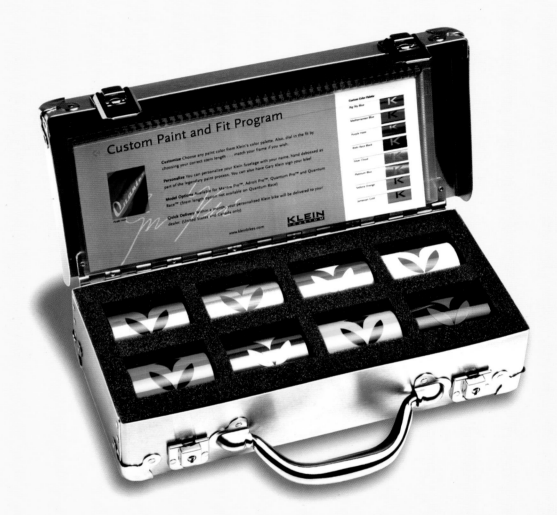

The stainless-steel case reminds dealers of the product design itself. It is sturdy, functional, and impressive-looking.

The Custom Paint Program Dealer Toolkit is a metal case of finish samples that dealers can use to demonstrate options to their customers. The painted samples give customers a much truer idea of the richness and depth of the bike colors than a printed swatch book could.

The Klein Catalog cover features the fourteen custom colors and ten international flag colors that are available on the bikes.

Catalog pages show product details, spotlighting the work of Gary Klein, the MIT engineer and inventor/designer of the bicycles. Color is used as an attractor to convey brand benefits by illustrating the many color choices available in a variety of Klein products.

Design Firm:

Mevis & Van Deursen

Los Amorales **by Carlos Amorales**
Client: Artimo

Los Amorales is a book about a coherent series of works by the Mexican artist Carlos Amorales. The book was commissioned by the publisher Artimo and edited by Mevis & Van Deursen in collaboration with the artist. It chronicles an art project in a series of snapshot-like images and large, raw typography.

Amorales, working with professional fighters, organized Mexican wrestling matches in museums and art institutions. The wrestlers normally dressed like comic book heroes, but Amorales had them wear suits and masks based on a portrait of the artist. The book documents the behind-the-scenes story of meeting the wrestlers, creating the masks, and finally staging the wrestling matches.

▲ The brutality of the typography, and its red color, refer to authentic street posters that typically announce Mexican wrestling matches. Captions appear large on the pages of the book, making them manifest and adding to the impact.

◀

The book was printed partially in four-color process and partly in spot color to keep costs down. However, the use of color became a deliberate way to mark the sections of the book and keep the Mexican wrestling vernacular. The back cover features an iconic illustration of a Mexican wrestling mask.

F*** Amorales

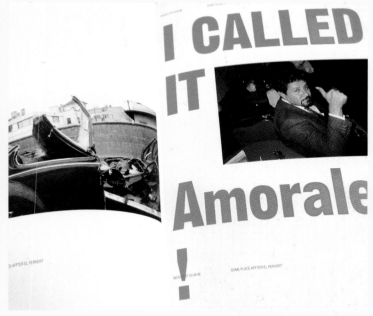

I CALLED IT Amorale !

IT WAS A SHOCKING IMAGE

THE FIRST I HAD OF AMORALES AS A LIVING PERSON

SAN DIEGO

WYNDHAM EMERALD PLAZA HOTEL

20 JANUARY 2000 — 20:00 HRS

Design Firm:

Motion Theory

Hewlett Packard Anthem
Client: Goodby Silverstein & Partners, Hewlett Packard

With the merge of digital giants HP and Compaq, HP and its advertising agency sought to communicate the unique advantages of the new company to business and retail customers with a major television campaign. The concept "+hp" shows how HP works with its customers to empower their businesses.

The strategy was to create simple yet powerful graphic design laid over film images from a variety of fields in which HP's products have made a difference. The visual motif of a + sign followed by the HP logo interacts with environments symbolizing innovation and achievement in various business, scientific, and artistic situations.

A challenge of this campaign was unifying many types of business thematically. Color is used in a subdued and subtle way, as in this dreamy, desaturated landscape shot.

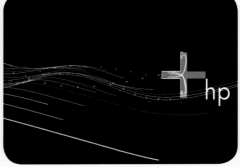

The "+hp" treatment was introduced into each scene to represent the contributions HP makes to its customers, including the online retailer Amazon.com. The + symbol appears in bright hues of red, blue, green, and yellow, floating through the Amazon business environment image.

Graphics in spectrum colors animate across black backgrounds, working to transition the narrative parts of the spots. Although the lines of colors are bright, they are used in a minimal way to punctuate the + signs streaming across the background.

Simple typography clearly conveys the benefits of the newly merged HP in an elegant visual solution. The lines of spectrum color even out at the top and bottom of the screen to frame the typography and emphasize the message.

bang & olufsen +hp

The campaign challenged the designers to create meaning using little more than movement, color, and the placement of the +hp device. The restrained use of minimal, brightly colored graphic elements, such as the lines and +, move across subtly colored photographic images to create a fine art quality to the television spots.

Design Firm:

The *New York Times Magazine*

The New York Issue Publication Design
Client: The *New York Times Magazine*

The designers were charged with a brief to visualize a design for the annual "New York" issue of the *New York Times Magazine* that spoke to that year's topic: the arts and culture. The design needed to clearly communicate "special issue," setting itself apart from the regular Sunday version while retaining the magazine's identity.

The approach to the project was to view the issue as a gallery or museum exhibition translated into the form of a magazine, taking design cues from the design and graphics used in these environments. The cover, shown below, introduces a gallery space, and the theme continues throughout the issue with a signage-inspired structure for the typography. Environmental signage and wayfinding systems inspired the movement of all display type to a horizontal structure hanging from the top of the page.

Inspired by exhibitions, the designers introduced the issue with an almost structural three-dimensional space on the cover.

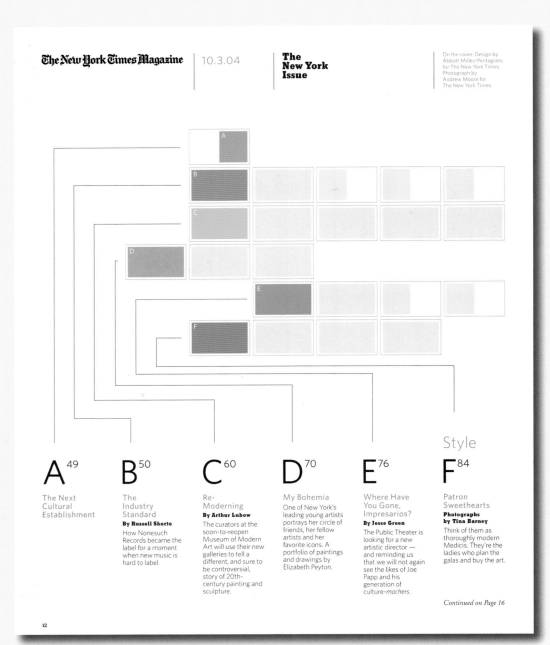

The New York Times Magazine   10.3.04   The New York Issue

On the cover: Design by Abbott Miller/Pentagram, for The New York Times. Photograph by Andrew Moore for The New York Times.

Style

A 49
The Next Cultural Establishment

B 50
The Industry Standard
By Russell Shorto
How Nonesuch Records became the label for a moment when new music is hard to label.

C 60
Re-Moderning
By Arthur Lubow
The curators at the soon-to-reopen Museum of Modern Art will use their new galleries to tell a different, and sure to be controversial, story of 20th-century painting and sculpture.

D 70
My Bohemia
One of New York's leading young artists portrays her circle of friends, her fellow artists and her favorite icons. A portfolio of paintings and drawings by Elizabeth Peyton.

E 76
Where Have You Gone, Impresarios?
By Jesse Green
The Public Theater is looking for a new artistic director — and reminding us that we will not again see the likes of Joe Papp and his generation of culture-machers.

F 84
Patron Sweethearts
Photographs by Tina Barney
Think of them as thoroughly modern Medicis. They're the ladies who plan the galas and buy the art.

Continued on Page 16

12

Style | **Patron Sweethearts**

Think of them as thoroughly modern Medicis. They're the ladies who plan the galas and buy the art.

F⁸⁴

PHOTOGRAPHS BY
TINA BARNEY

TEXT: MAURA EGAN
FASHION EDITOR:
ANNE CHRISTENSEN

THE FALL, for Manhattan's young Medici types, can be grueling — with galas and openings and armory-size antiques-fests clogging up the social calendar well into winter. This year, supporting the arts has become an Olympic sport — not only in nurturing the city's emerging talent but also in campaigning for the millions (and millions) of dollars needed to finance shiny monuments like Yoshio Taniguchi's 630,000-square-foot glass-and-granite expansion of the Museum of Modern Art or the New Museum of Contemporary Art's future home on the Bowery, which will soon break ground. All of this at a moment of pre-election jitters in a cash-strapped city. Who has the money, interest or energy to help something as abstract as art? These New York women. They are not Bergdorf blondes looking for a cause between collagen injections and lunch at Le Cirque. These ladies are the behind-the-scene movers and shakers, planning the parties, picking the art and making sure that the museums are as vibrant as the work that hangs on their walls.

Allison Sarofim comes from a family of art lovers: her mother, Louisa, is the board president of the Menil Collection in Houston; her father, Fayez (Forbes calls him "the buy-and-hold king"), seems to single-handedly prop up most of Texas' cultural institutions. Sarofim, 33, was an intern at the Menil before joining the Young Collectors Council at the Guggenheim, which has an actual say in what the museum acquires, having gambled on the likes of Anna Gaskell and Thomas Demand. Sarofim's own collection includes the Rothko over the fireplace. Zac Posen dress, $1,600. At Barneys New York. Christian Louboutin shoes. Fred Leighton jewelry.

84 SAROFIM'S HAIR BY EVELYN CALDERON AND MAKEUP BY IVETTE GIL, BOTH FOR BUTTERFLY STUDIO

A blueprint of this issue appears on the Table of Contents, at left. Each feature is represented by a series of colored rectangles, which symbolize a magazine spread. This map graphic is apparent on the opener of each feature, see right.

A map graphic was used as a navigational device, with color delineating each feature story. Colors shift as the reader progresses through the magazine.

The Industry Standard

B⁵⁰

PHOTOGRAPHS BY
JEFF RIEDEL

Design Firm:

Segura Inc.

Segura, Inc., developed the 5inch brand of CDs and cases as an alternative to drab and dull ready-made CDs and time-consuming, expensive custom labels. These predesigned silk-screened blanks are available in CD-R and DVD-R formats and are suitable for storing all kinds of data, from design projects to music. 5inch also offers unique CD cases, storage products, and wearables.

As a subsidiary of Segura, Inc., the designers became, in a sense, their own clients in developing both the products and the marketing efforts to support them. 5inch products stand out because of bright colors used in well-designed graphic patterns and illustrations in a range of artistic styles.

5inch Custom-Designed CD-Rs and Cases
Client: 5inch

5inch CDs are available in an ever evolving variety of choices. There are CDs that look like classic composition notebooks with their distinctive marbled pattern, a crowd of flat doll-like figures set against a bright yellow background, and a cropped U.S. flag of red, white, and blue. Segura is constantly launching new CD products featuring unique and colorful designs in styles from contemporary to retro.

5inch CDs feature a variety of graphic treatments for the discs, housed in unique flip-top cases. Each disc uses color and graphics in a distinctive manner. From

yellow ruled "paper" reminiscent of a legal pad to an icy blue and silver takeoff on a disco ball, each design conveys a particular mood and concept.

5inch offers consumers an alternative to standard blank CDs. Color and design are key reasons to purchase these products.

Design Firm:

Stripe (Jon Sueda/Gail Swanlund)

Googie Redux: Ultramodern Roadside Architecture, by Alan Hess
Client: Chronicle Books

The project tasked to Stripe was to redesign the book *Googie: Fifties Coffee Shop Architecture,* originally published in 1985. The redesign moves the book away from a pop culture souvenir book by treating the material as an architectural treatise. *Googie Redux* features the unconventional architecture of coffee shops and drive-in diners located primarily in Los Angeles in the 1950s.

The exaggerated forms of Googie structures were created to grab the attention of motorists. Each neon sign, angular glass, and thematic structure acted as a huge advertisement for the establishment it represented. The design of the book embraced the idea of experiencing the architecture from a moving car. The extreme scale used on the typographic openers, the mortised shapes of the photographs, and the layout grid all mimic the Googie aesthetic.

▲ Large display typography, photo shapes, and a variety of graphic icons used throughout the book mimic a Googie itself.

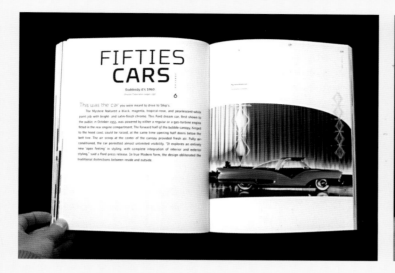

The dominant color themes in the book include a range of sun-bleached Formica colors inspired by the images of the Googie diners. Color was used pragmatically to differentiate the sections of the book. Fields of color often underlie blocks of text, enlivening black-and-white spreads, as seen right. The more than twenty typefaces used in *Googie Redux* represent the diversity of typographic forms in the urban landscape.

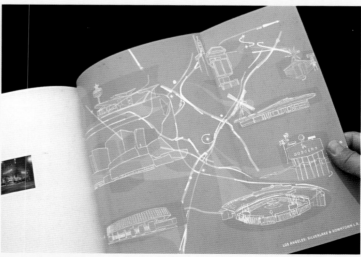

Old photographs provide the majority of the color in the book. Taking cues from these images, the design utilizes pale blue and gold as accents.

The inside covers feature a map of Googie structures in Los Angeles. The blue color simulates the look of an architectural blueprint.

Design Firm:

Andrea Tinnes

"Tage Des Deutschen Films in Tbilissi" Film Festival Posters (2002–2004)
Client: Medea: Film/Production/Service

This series of bilingual posters promotes the German Film Festival/Tbilissi in Georgia, a former Soviet republic, and Germany. The posters illustrate the concept of cultural exchange with basic graphic elements. The circles are a metaphor for film projection and symbolize the fusion of ideas.

The design of the posters over the three-year span shown here reference the visual language historically used in movie posters. The design also pays homage to the visual language of Russian Constructivism and the aesthetics that represent revolution. The focal points, or centers of the design, feature an image characteristic of Georgia.

Georgia's language uses a different alphabet than German. The designer, Andrea Tinnes, created a modern Georgian typeface, Avaza Mtavruli, that works well aesthetically with the Spektro Gothic typeface she designed for the German text. The typography works with the bold, predominantly primary colors to attract the eye and promote the film festival. The designs for the first two posters are virtually the same, with the color scheme shift being the primary change. Tinnes used high-contrast colors—black and yellow—as backgrounds to attract attention to the festival graphics.

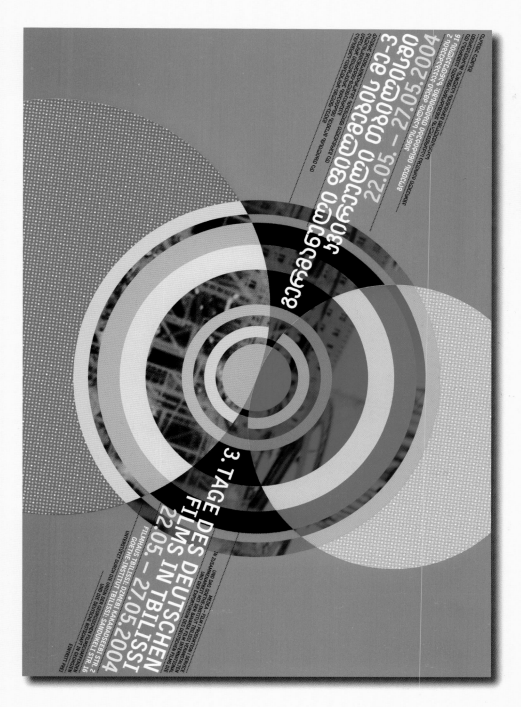

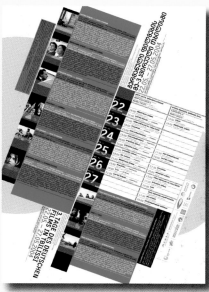

The 2004 festival poster uses red to reference the political Rose Revolution experienced in Georgia, formerly part of the Soviet Union. The poster back, above, is a program schedule. Budget constraints prompted the use of only two colors, but the designer achieved beautiful results. The use of alternating paragraphs with black and white type on blocks of medium blue creates the impression of more colors. Photographic images handled in duotones look rich and provide additional depth to the layout.

Design Firm:

Walker Art Center

How Latitudes Become Forms **Exhibition Catalogue**
Client: Walker Art Center

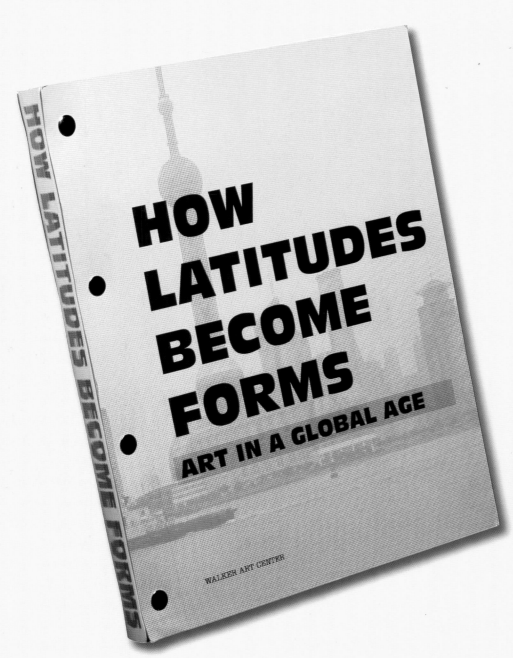

This catalog documents How Latitudes Become Forms, the Walker Art Center's four-year global initiative, and its culminating exhibition, which explores a variety of international artists working in media ranging from painting and sculpture to video and performance. It acts as an alternative to the traditional exhibition catalog, reflecting the show's transient, humble aesthetic.

The catalog features a utilitarian design and straightforward construction, which references the form and visual strategies of a research document. The components of the book are color-coded: essays are light blue, conversations are pink, writings are on pale yellow, and artists' works are reproduced on white.

The catalog is softcovered and postbound, enhancing its presentation as a compiled research document. This type of binding also allows the title of the catalog to be edge-printed on the spine. The cover design features a muted photographic image reproduced in a soft orange-peach color that contrasts with the bold black type. The yellow orange rectangular shape behind the copy "Art in a Global Age" highlights the show's tagline.

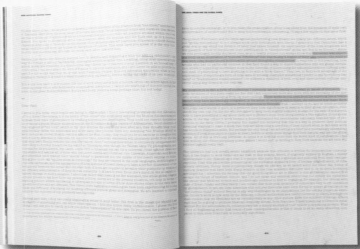

Selected writings were photocopied directly from their original sources and redacted, their accompanying illustrations sometimes blacked out for copyright purposes. The catalog references a research journal by highlighting passages of text in essays and conversations, as seen above.

Color is used to code the sections of the catalog, unifying content such as written conversations, essays, travel snapshots, and artists' works collected over a four-year initiative. The background colors tend to reference common color paper stock sheets used in research documents.

**Chapter 6:
Color Talk**

Many designers have difficulty articulating the rationale behind their color systems. At times, this is a result of having chosen a particular palette out of instinct. Choices made intuitively are hard to verbalize. In other instances, language for discussing the subtleties of tints and shades of hues and various color interactions simply escapes them. Nevertheless, talking about color with clients remains an important part of the design process.

"If one says "red" (the name of the color) and there are fifty people listening, it can be expected that there will be fifty reds in their minds. And one can be sure that all these reds will be very different."
—Josef Albers

What is your favorite color, and why?
The pattern shown opposite is composed of the favorite colors of the people who worked together to create this book. They answered the question, "What is your favorite color, and why?" This is a simple demonstration of how different people talk about color. It seems that talking about color brings out the poet in nearly everyone.

1. "Aqua blue. It's not green and not blue, but somewhere between. It's cool and clear like a swimming pool."
—Sean Adams

2. "Green. It means life and newness."
—Noreen Morioka

3. "Blue. It is optimistic and full of potential."
—Rudi Adrian Tcruz

4. "Red. It's emotional."
—Volker Dürre

5. "My favorite color has been, and will always be, blue. I really don't think I can attach any kind of logic as to why. There are certain shades of blue (teal and midnight blue) that, when I see them, I am immediately drawn to them. It could be an object, a photo, anything—if it's in this color, I am in love."
—Victoria Lam

6. "Phthalo blue. It's the color of "blue water," the ocean far out at sea."
—Kristin Ellison

7. "Purple, for its richness and surprise. It is both cold and warm. It is the color that my mind fills with when I eat chocolate, touch velvet, or feel a cool refreshing wind against my face."
—Cynthia Jacquette

8. "I like green, especially sage, avocado, and chartreuse. Greens are both lively and relaxing."
—Terry Stone

9. "Black. It's the most honest."
—Scott Meisse

10. "My favorite color has always been blue. Preferably a deep, dark, neutralized blue. I like this blue because it is the color of the night sky in van Gogh's *Starry Night*, and when I see it I'm there, warmed by the kindly glow of the stars."
—Brody Larson

11. "My favorite is black, but that technically is not a color, right? So I would then say red."
—David Martinell

12. "Blue/green—can I say that? and why? Color of the ocean."
—Cora Hawks

1. Sean Adams

2. Noreen Morioka

3. Rudi Adrian Tcruz

4. Volker Dürre

7. Cynthia Jacuette

6. Kristin Ellison

10. Brody Larson

11. David Martinell

9. Scott Meisse

12. Cora Hawks

5. Victoria Lam

8. Terry Stone

Talking About Color in Design

Talking about color will always be a challenge. Colors are associated with emotional states, symbolism, cultural meanings, and aesthetic preferences—all of which are deeply personal and experientially specific to the viewer. In addition, color terms do vary from culture to culture but also the language itself constantly evolves. For example, a language may start out with one or two names for blue and develop hundreds of names to describe ever more specific variations on the hue blue.

Associations Help Determine Color Names

Color names are linguistic labels that humans attach to hues. Hues are determined by the physics of light reflection. The most dominant wavelength that is apparent is what gets named. Despite the complex systems that determine a color, most colors are named by association—either relative position on the color wheel, as in blue-green, or by reference to some natural object of that hue, such as the gemstone turquoise. Both terms can be used to describe the same hue. Changes in saturation can be expressed by adding a modifying label to the name, as in vivid turquoise. To describe changes in value, we generally add a reference to intensity, as in light turquoise or dark blue-green. Special kinds of reflection provide additional modification, like metallic turquoise, sparkling blue green, and opalescent aqua.

Use of standardized color systems provides nomenclature for colors, as in the PANTONE® PMS names or Munsell's alphanumeric lexicon. However valuable and important it is to refer to colors in this manner during production, it is of little use in describing colors in conversations with clients. With all these variations in the language of color, the designer's best strategy for talking about color is simply to show it. Showing the entire proposed color system by applying it to various types of materials illustrates how the colors interact and provides confirmation that the designer has thought through color systematically. The choice of color seems far less arbitrary and therefore is more likely to meet with client approval.

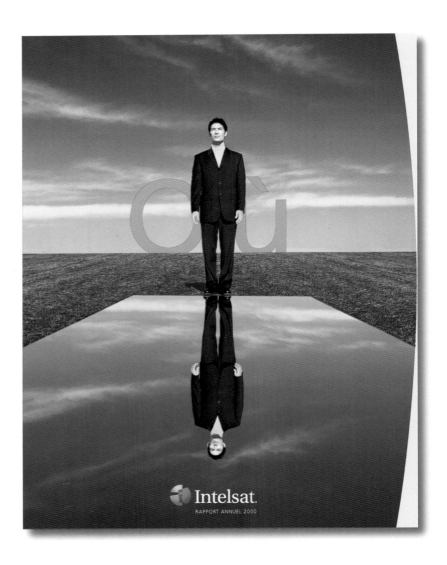

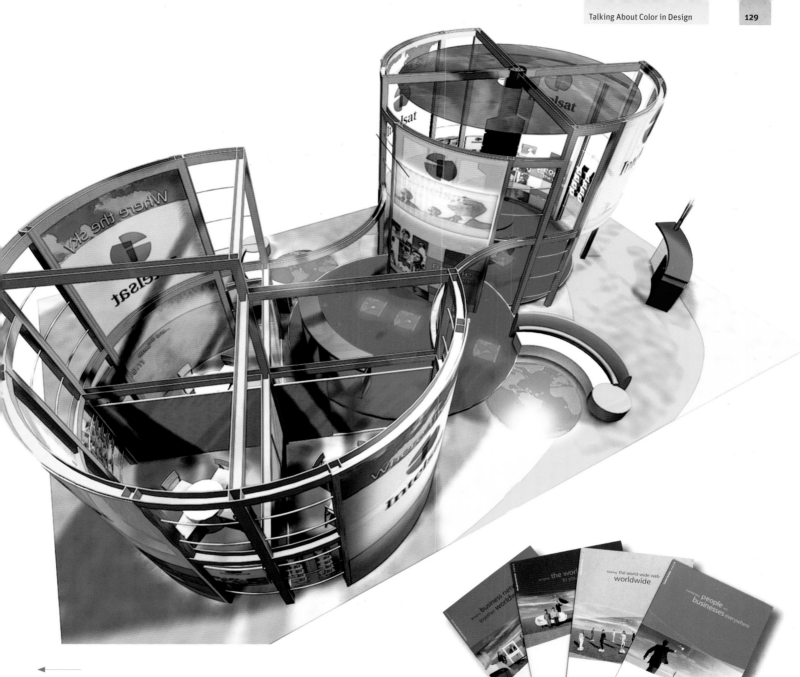

In working with Intelesat, a communications company, the designers at Addison demonstrated full usage of a range of colors. The analogous color scheme of blues, teals, and greens is shown in thematic illustrative photos, corporate literature, signage, and trade exhibition structures, as seen at right and opposite. This type of presentation allows designers to speak of color in a cohesive manner. When the designer uses the word "blue" the client understands which blue and how it will be used. **Addison Company**

AIGA

Competitions & Exhibitions   National Design Center

In both the television spot for Adidas, left, and the AIGA poster, above, color is an integral part of the concept of the piece. In the case of Adidas, the spot shows the new color palette for the products in an interesting yet simple approach. Since Adidas owns the three stripes that are part of its logo, the designers take advantage of the equity by bringing them to life and using them to guide the viewer through the swatch palette. In the AIGA poster, a list of design competition categories is typeset in colors that overlap, interact, and vibrate while providing a metaphor for the wealth of visual information types in graphic design.

Brand New School, Adidas
Chermayeff & Geismar, AIGA

Color Names

What's in a name? Searching for a way to describe that specific color in your layout? Here are some suggestions for descriptive color names:

Reds	**Blues**	**Greens**	**Blacks**
Alizarin crimson	Aqua	Avocado	Anthracite
Berry	Azure	Cactus	Carbon
Blood	Baby	Celadon	Ebony
Brick	Blueberry	Celery	Jet
Burgundy	Cadet	Chartreuse	Lamp black
Cadmium red	Cerulean	Citron	Licorice
Candy apple	Cobalt	Cucumber	Obsidian
Cherry	Cornflower	Emerald	Onyx
Chili	Cyan	Fern	
Cinnabar	Indigo	Forest	**Whites**
Claret	Lapis	Grass	Alabaster
Crimson	Midnight	Honeydew	Antique white
Dusty rose	Peacock	Hunter	Coconut
Flame	Periwinkle	Jade	Cream
Magenta	Prussian	Kelly	Ecru
Maroon	Reflex	Leaf	Eggshell
Merlot	Robin's egg	Lime	Ghost
Paprika	Royal	Mint	Glacier
Pink	Sapphire	Moss	Ice
Raspberry	Sea	Nile	Ivory
Rose	Sky	Olive	Linen
Rose madder	Steel	Pear	Pearl
Rouge	Surf	Pine	Porcelain
Ruby	Teal	Pistachio	Snow
Sangria	Turquoise	Sage	Titanium white
Scarlet	Ultramarine	Sap	Vanilla
Strawberry		Seafoam	
Terra-cotta	**Oranges**	Spring	**Grays**
Tomato	Apricot	Terre verte	Ash
Wine	Carrot	Viridian	Chrome
	Citrus		Fawn
Yellows	Copper	**Purples**	Mist
Amber	Coral	Amethyst	Nickel
Banana	Marmalade	Aubergine	Pewter
Butter	Peach	Blackberry	Silver
Cheddar	Persimmon	Eggplant	Slate
Cornsilk	Pumpkin	Fuchsia	Smoke
Daffodil	Salmon	Grape	Steel
Gold	Tangerine	Heather	Stone
Goldenrod		Hyacinth	
Lemon		Hydrangea	
Marigold		Iris	
Mustard		Lavender	
Nugget		Lilac	
Ochre		Mauve	
Sun		Orchid	
Sunflower		Plum	
		Puce	
		Thistle	
		Violet	

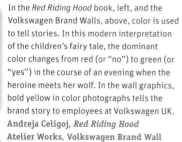

In the *Red Riding Hood* book, left, and the Volkswagen Brand Walls, above, color is used to tell stories. In this modern interpretation of the children's fairy tale, the dominant color changes from red (or "no") to green (or "yes") in the course of an evening when the heroine meets her wolf. In the wall graphics, bold yellow in color photographs tells the brand story to employees at Volkswagen UK.

Andreja Celigoj, *Red Riding Hood*
Atelier Works, Volkswagen Brand Wall

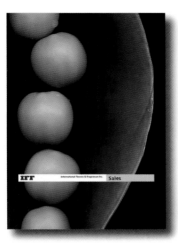

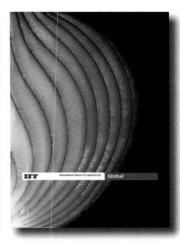

The colors of nature were used to tell the story of *Nature Unveiled* and reposition the chemical giant International Flavors & Fragrances. The company was perceived as old and stodgy, so the designers created a fresh approach. Rather than focus on the end product, which is mass manufactured and distributed by a large corporation, the designers built the brand around nature, the source of these products. Close-up photographs of flowers and fruits create a softer story for the company, as seen here in brochures and package design.
Powell

Presenting Color to Clients

Set the tone for a great working relationship with clients in terms of color. We recommend the following tips to help get your color choices approved:

Get Input Up Front

- Survey your client about color when you start a project. Ask if they have ideas about color usage. Make sure you understand why they may or may not be tied to these preferences.
- Get the client's corporate identity colors in CMYK, RGB, and spot color values to avoid guesswork.

Please Yourself

- Keeping in mind a client's objectives and input, concentrate on designing to your own high standards and selecting the colors that work best within given parameters.
- Creativity, and especially color usage, is subjective. However, do develop a rationale for why you have selected a particular palette.

Limit Choices

- Present only your favorite color solutions and an alternative. Too many creative choices are confusing and convey the impression that you are indecisive.

Control the Presentation

- Show the color scheme in a variety of applications. If required, show color in print and on the screen. Seeing color in action makes it clearer and easier for a client to approve.
- Summarize the client's input and objectives. Explain why these colors, along with the other design elements, meet the project objectives and are the best choice.
- Involve the client in a discussion about color only relative to their objectives. Challenge revisions that will not meet the objectives effectively; accept changes that will.

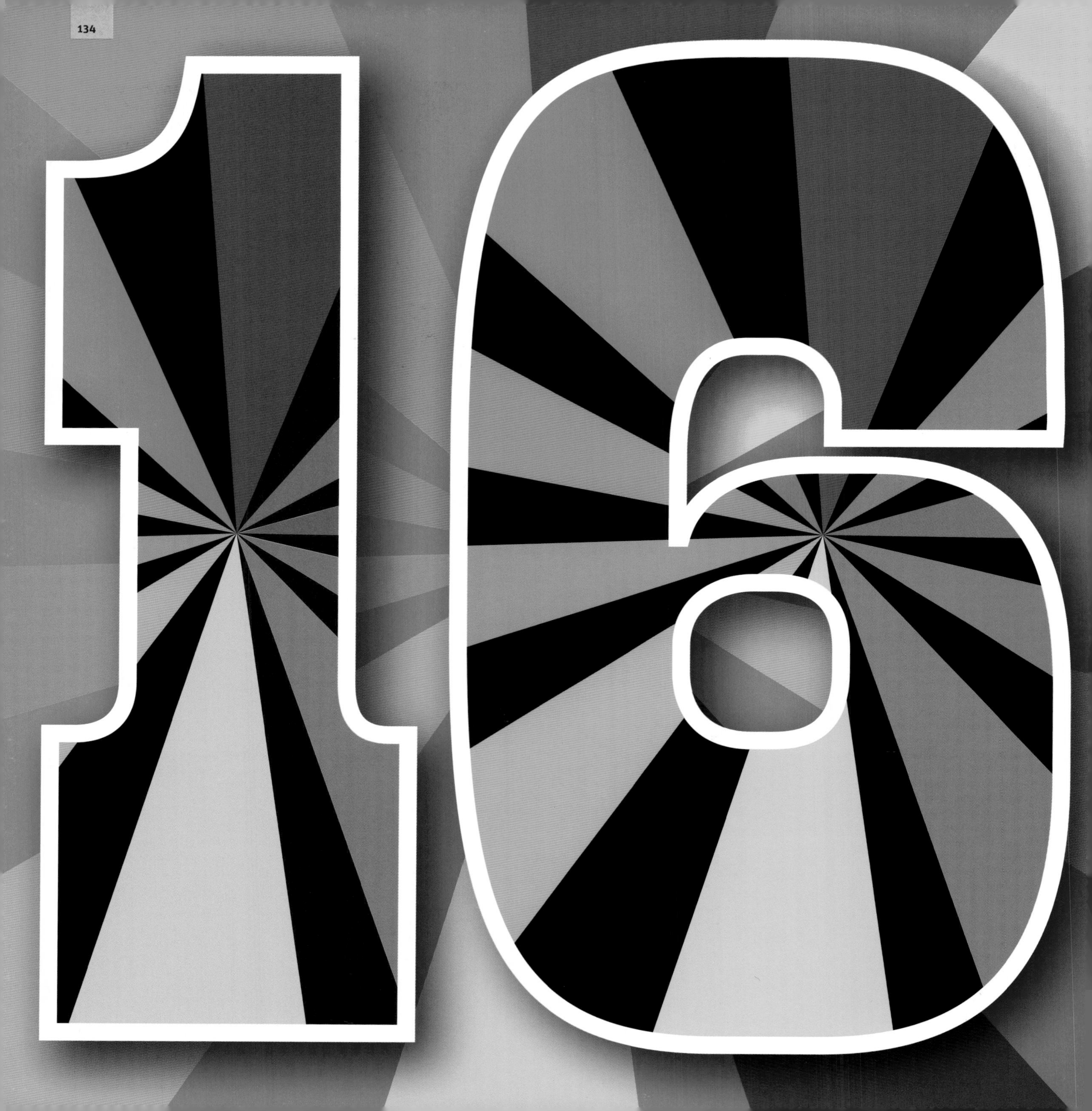
16

Case Studies

For this book, AdamsMorioka decided to approach case studies by examining the work of sixteen internationally diverse design firms. We asked this group of talented designers to share their philosophies and processes as well as information about their aesthetic preferences. In every instance, these designers have won industry recognition through awards and accolades of all types. To find out more about their companies, please see the index of contributors.

AdamsMorioka

Beverly Hills, USA

AdamsMorioka is interested in prescient vision pared down to its most direct and powerful level. Formed in 1994 by partners Sean Adams and Noreen Morioka, the firm's ideas of clarity and purity have led a revolution in design away from complexity, chaos, and dystopia toward simplicity and utopia. The designers' definition of simplicity involves using the most salient and minimal forms to communicate. AdamsMorioka aims to eliminate visual clutter and provide designs that are smart and unexpected.

The firm's work is intended to be understood and resonate with multiple audiences, not just visually sophisticated designers. "We think the message should be clear and memorable, the experience should be entertaining and engaging, and the viewer should be spoken to with respect," explains Sean Adams. There is a genuinely optimistic attitude that runs through all of AdamsMorioka's work.

This point of view is very much in evidence in AdamsMorioka's use of color. There is a preference for colors that are pure and accessible. In a formal sense, color is used to create maximum contrast. Most colors are strong, with pastels used rarely or only as accents dominated by the bolder hues.

Philosophically, AdamsMorioka uses color to seduce audiences into the subject of the piece. "Typically, color is used to convey the client's primary message or to provide access into it. At other times, color is used as a stage set or veneer in that from a distance the piece appears to be one thing, then on closer inspection more and different layers of meaning are revealed," explains Adams.

The cover for the University of California at Los Angeles Extension catalog is a twist on autumn imagery. The design features stripes of new versions of traditional fall colors—burnt orange, greens, taupes, browns, and golds. Images include a fallen leaf iconic of autumn, a pencil representing "back to school," and an open book, symbolic of education but skewed because it contains a manipulated photo of a swimming pool—all of which say that autumn in Los Angeles is like no place else.

UCLA Summer Sessions 1998
www.summer.ucla.edu

Again, color is utilized to represent the season. As with the piece on the previous page, the design includes iconic imagery of Los Angeles. This UCLA Extension Catalog cover captures a beach scene similar to those seen in movies and television. The summer sky and several vertical surfboards standing in the sand are a well-known image of Malibu, this time done in a posterized serigraphic style. The color is not exact but rather an expressive representation of the intensity of the light during this time of year.

Summer is pared down to its essence in this UCLA Extension Catalog cover commissioned by UCLA creative director Inju Sturgeon. Pure color is used to capture the heat of the season. A flat symbolic plane of yellow, a sliver of blue ocean, and a fiery orange sun in a white sky are UCLA's school colors. The orange is also a traditional symbol of Los Angeles. This piece is a good example of what famed CalArts professor Ed Fella refers to as "AdamsMorioka's habit of putting more into less in their designs."

Being located in Los Angeles affects AdamsMorioka's choice of colors. "We're in southern California, and the quality of light is bright; our colors are saturated. We have light powering in through the windows—it is a bright and vibrant place." When AdamsMorioka's work is transported to other cities, it really stands out. Lively colors contrast with gray environments in places such as New York, making the firm's color schemes jump out and get noticed.

When asked why so many pieces designed by AdamsMorioka are pink, Adams replied, "I love pink, vibrant pinks and fuchsias. I like it because it is optimistic and pleasant, and it allows us to get away with murder. We design projects in pink that others tend to do in stark black and white. They get into trouble for glorifying tough subject matter, while our designs get accepted. Only later do people realize that AdamsMorioka has used the same iconography with strong messaging. It's just wrapped in a different palette."

Color is a psychological tool. It is not a fashion or trend to AdamsMorioka. However, Adams adds, "Left to my own devices, my color palettes would be very Pop Art. Noreen brings in the Asian influence and keeps us in check. She transforms palettes to be more sophisticated and refined."

Adams and Morioka have many speaking and judging engagements annually, and a pleasure associated with these commitments is designing the announcement posters. This poster is for a lecture in Tulsa, Oklahoma (OK). AdamsMorioka (AM) and OK together reads "AMOK," an interesting idea in and of itself. Dominated by medium hot pink adjacent to a rich ochre, the piece features classic retro images including the Theme Building at LAX, canned pineapple rings, Hostess Snowball cakes, and two vintage hunting textile patterns.

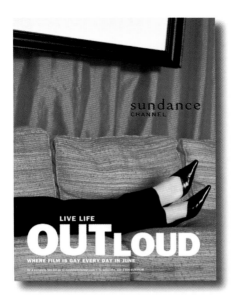

"I just refuse to choose ugly colors. I want to use colors that show the world as the best it can possibly be." —Sean Adams

These ads promote Sundance Channel Television Network's programming block called "Out Loud," a presentation of gay-themed movies. The slogan "Where Film Is Gay Every Day in June" is demonstrated through a variety of images with fuchsia backgrounds. The idea, living out loud and gay, is represented by the hot pink. These photos play off of gay stereotypes, turning them on their heads.

This *Appleton Exhibition* catalog cover features the colors perhaps most associated with AdamsMorioka—pink and orange. The fused metaphor concept of two seemingly unrelated photographs placed side by side, in this case a "Modern and Church Models" piano juxtaposed with a hand holding a gun pointed directly at the viewer, is an unsettling image greatly softened by the color scheme.

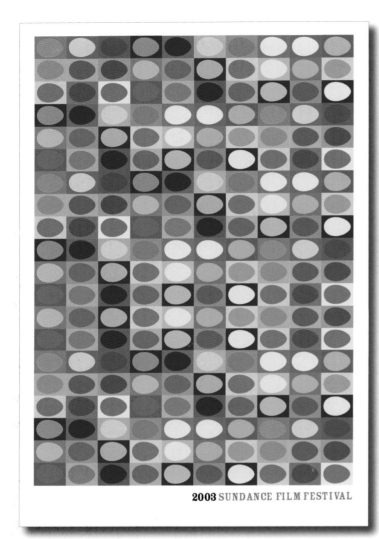

2003 SUNDANCE FILM FESTIVAL

The Sundance Film Festival, the premiere venue for independent films, is held in Park City, Utah, each January, making it the first major U.S. film festival of each year. AdamsMorioka has been engaged to create the brand identity, including logo, marketing, promotional, and environmental graphics, since 2003. Over time, the festival has become more and more strongly yet simply identified. Above is a special-edition festival poster featuring an unusual palette of pastel colors in a mini egg pattern.

This poster for the 2004 festival is the most sought-after to date. Illustrator Robert Sherrill collaborated with AdamsMorioka to create a true Old West icon—the cowboy. The yellow, amber, and brown color scheme is a metaphor for the golden west and Utah, where Sundance takes place.

2005 Sundance Film Festival
Park City, Utah • January 20–30, 2005

The Film Guide for the 2005 Sundance Film Festival features bold use of a warm red on the cover. Several layers of images overlap to reference narrative film structure. Typography takes its cues from the lettering on actual film stock and suggests movement over time with the slight blurring of the letterforms.

The 2005 poster captures the idea of snow with its large white background subtly varnished with a faint pattern. Sundance is a winter festival at which audiences often must deal with snowy conditions. The lone figure pulling a red strip of film through the vast white field is a metaphor for the indie filmmaker bringing his or her film to audiences in a lonely but energetic battle against the odds.

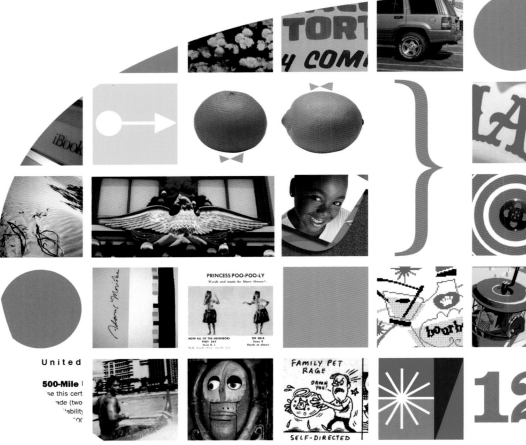

This poster designed for a speaking engagement for AIGA Portland captures the attitude and style of AdamsMorioka through a series of images of AdamsMorioka projects, inspirations, and the environment at AdamsMorioka. Contained within an oval shape to suggest the world, the simple, bright, and optimistic palette was chosen to complement the images and act as a counterpoint to the title, "The Scary World."

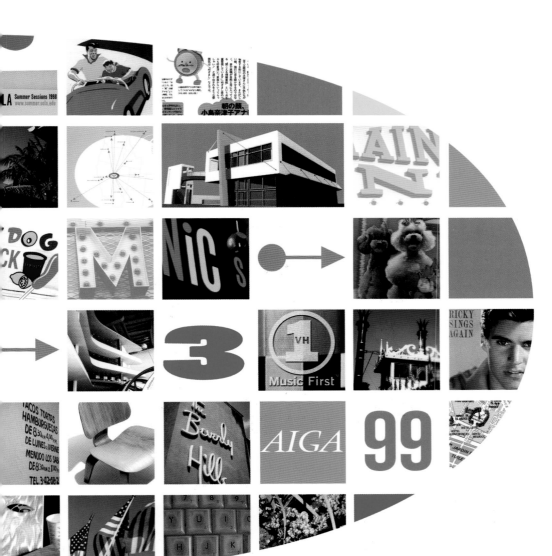

The scary world of **AdamsMorioka**

AIGA Portland presents Sean Adams

Friday, December 3, 1999 • 6–9:00pm • Presentation 8:00pm

Portland Art Museum • 1219 SW Park Avenue

Brand New School
Santa Monica/New York, USA

Brand New School (BNS), a live action and design company, responds to visual culture all over the world, translating it into television commercials, music videos, and on-air network identity packages. BNS has evolved in a very short time from boutique shop to major player in on-air television broadcast design and commercial production. Founded in 2000 by Jonathan Notaro, later joined by typography master Jens Gehlhaar, the firm has offices on both U.S. coasts.

Notaro founded BNS to be a creative boutique that he describes as "a bit off center, where we're comfortable." He is determined to create a new school of thought that extends design beyond a mere typographical experience. The firm is immersed in visual style in both printed media and motion pictures, and the designers are deeply aware of the importance of knowing how the viewer is affected. Notaro says, "The key is to put together a group of creative people, give them the freedom to do their thing, and keep it fun, even during ninety-hour weeks."

The play principle may be key, and the work exhibits strong innovation. BNS has successfully negotiated a tough balancing act between the demands of advertising clients and producing thoughtful, striking work. "As graphic designers, we're telling a story, and at the end of the day, it's more involving to see performance than flying type." One of the key elements used in BNS narratives is color.

This was Mudd Jeans' first commercial, which aired exclusively on MTV. Meant to appeal to teenage girls, the spot communicates the large variety of washes and textures available. BNS shot a dancing model in front of a green screen. Later everything was erased but the jeans. The pants appear to take a journey through fantastic environments in a cross between a storybook cartoon world and a hip dance video. The various environments dictated the color palettes, all highly saturated and using the full spectrum of color.

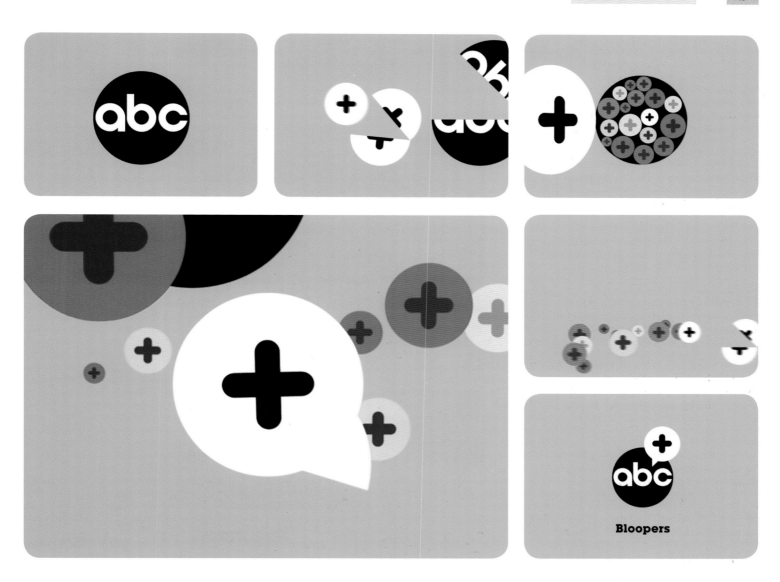

BNS created this show package for ABC TV's new evening programming look. The piece visually illustrates "the idea of getting more from the evening than you'd expect" by playing off the circle shape of the logo.

The simple animation of the logo, circles, a talk bubble, and a plus sign have an interesting personality. A bright, playful palette of high-key colors is used, with a bright lime green background chosen because of its contrast with the ABC trademark colors of black and, alternatively, bright international yellow. The green conveys the message of a variety of television content and is refreshingly different as an on-air ID for the network.

"We really don't have a color philosophy. I guess our use of color started as being a bit more pop-ish and fun rather than muted and serious," explains Jonathan Notaro. "Subtleties in color don't necessarily translate well on television." So BNS' color choices tend to be brighter colored. Notaro continues, "This is partly due to the amount of humor in our work. A brighter palette seems to enforce that not-so-serious attitude."

Brand New School tends toward a more optimistic color palette that is hip and masculine. Pop culture elements are fused with parody modes of contemporary art. All design aspects reflect the contradictory ideas of modern life. "I think we have a deeper understanding of design history than many companies that evolved from street culture," creative director Gelhaar comments, "which keeps the work as intelligent as it is creative."

While conceptually driven, theirs is a highly technical as well as aesthetically demanding medium. Notaro explains, "Most of the time we are concerned about getting our ideas figured out in terms of narrative and visual arts. This is due mainly to having short deadlines, and color usually isn't something that is heavily scrutinized. Colors are just about the last thing we think about, or should I say, are conscious of, on a project."

"The mysticism of the digital realm has been unveiled, so I think its design has become much easier. Or has it? It's always interesting to see what spills over from the other side, formally and conceptually."—Jonathan Notaro

This spot for Fox's Fuel TV Network creates an action-based film language that is visually stunning. The spot recontextualizes an old movie genre. In B-movie style, a helmeted biker and his pack of Motocrossers rid the world of giant ant aliens before flying and stunting into the sunset, leaving mankind safe once more. The color palette is a desaturated 16mm grainy cheap-feeling film look. The image appears worn and damaged, with film angles mirroring the spirit of 1950s sci-fi. Matte painting, three-dimensional animation, and manipulated location photography all combine in a unique fusion of digital and analog.

For this music video, director Chris Appelbaum took the band American Hi-Fi to Hays, Kansas; threw a party at a fan's house; and let the cameras roll. With a punk rock attitude, BNS then designed five segments made to look like a high school student's scrapbook come to life. The piece explores rock and roll iconography without a tight graphic system; it is meant to seem made by multiple hands. The only structure imposed is the use of felt-tipped markers and ballpoint pens, which provide the color scheme as well.

Muse's "Hysteria" music video needed to be a breakthrough piece to reach American audiences. BNS created a performance video overlaid with graphic components that reinforce the lyrical content in this striking track. To match the hysteria of the song, brain abstraction graphics and visual hemorrhages of thought images leave the band submerged in a red cloud of bloodlike color. All color is desaturated, with skin tones preserved to make the band feel alive. Overall, the dark melancholic red creates an aggressive emotional feeling.

Brand New School developed a signature series of on-air identities for the Fuel Network. The designers thought it would be interesting to invite a celebrity surfer, skater, snowboarder, or Moto rider to collaborate with them to create unique limited-edition IDs. For this piece, BNS worked with Chris Pastras, a well-known graphic designer, artist, and illustrator in the skateboard industry. Chris turned over his sketchbooks, and BNS brought his sketches to life. The resulting piece talks about his heritage and influences as an artist. The color system was completely inspired by Chris's personal palette, which appears frequently in his works. The backgrounds are pale sepia brown, over which a variety of graphic elements, punctuated with bursts of bright color, are animated.

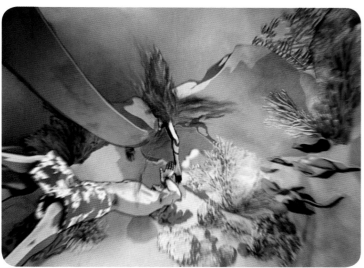

The only creative brief given was to generate something cool that promotes the action sports network Fuel. BNS developed a fairy-tale narrative about a surfer who is saved by a mermaid and discovers endless love in a beautiful undersea world. The hues are saturated and tropical. The piece was created digitally, without footage, and required a great deal of experimentation to create the feeling of an animated watercolor painting.

This network ID had to promote a contest targeting aspiring action sports filmmakers for Fuel. BNS used a long pan across a graphic landscape in the form of an abstracted editorial timeline that shows the process of crafting a film from start to premiere. The only colors used were black, white, and yellow, chosen for their simplicity and bold impact. This became the visual language for the Fuel Competition and all its related promotional materials.

Chimera Design
St. Kilda, Victoria, Australia

Chimera Design, established in 1997 by creative director John Magart, provides expertise for a diverse range of clients. The studio thrives on challenging projects and is focused on achieving unique outcomes in a diverse array of media. The designers constantly push the bounds of print and multimedia. Chimera believes that great design needs a strong conceptual base and point of difference. Color often provides the difference.

In response to questions about their color philosophy, designer Keelie Teasdale speaks for Chimera. "One's reaction to color is very personal and affected by social trends, styles, or conditioning, yet we as designers must create color combinations that have a concentrated impact on the majority of people." Chimera understands that changing color schemes in a particular design can create very different emotional responses. Teasdale continues, "Color defines the mood of the project. It subconsciously conveys the base feeling of the object you are designing for. It is the visual link to the core emotion of the job. It is imperative, therefore, to choose colors wisely."

"Color is one of the hardest design elements to constantly control. It's an ongoing battle of trial and error. When you get it right, the whole design falls into place."
—Keelie Teasdale

Tabcorp's introduction of a new betting game, *Mystery6,* into the Australian entertainment industry had to capture the carnival atmosphere of sporting fun, remain intriguing, and appeal to a broad market, especially the youth audience. The full-color logo, often placed on a black background, effectively relates to the name it accompanies. Shivering white in a spooky ghostlike fashion, the 6 hovers in the dark, surrounded by its energetic aura. Propelled off the page by magenta, its mysterious nature evokes festive excitement. The purple hues behind offer subtle hints of an ethereal nature, and it is these hues, often linked with good fortune and intuition, that add a sophistication and grounding to their dominant analogous partner.

The annual report for Dancehouse was an opportunity to create a document that matched the dynamic, innovative, and diverse nature of a progressive dance company. Needing to convey all the necessary requirements of a nonprofit organization's annual report and reflect the company's existing achromatic corporate image, the goal was to evoke contrary emotional reactions in the reader, much like that of a viewer of contemporary dance.

Fluorescent red, pale blue, and opaque white were chosen either to neutralize or intensify the corporate black throughout the piece. Printed over a mixture of four natural-toned stocks, the colors are intensified or subdued through their interaction with the paper. This combination of vivid, powerful red, often brash and almost assaulting; a refreshing pale blue, adding restraint; and a white that conveys calm through intricate detail create a pace within the book that exudes energy.

As each project's demands are different, Chimera believes it is impossible to work with a constant palette. "There are no rules to the amount of colors a job should use. Certain jobs demand full color usage, while others gain their impact from one carefully chosen spot color," says Teasdale. "Our key to choosing colors is breaking down the brief to its key emotional values. These points can be translated into their color equivalents. Depending on the desired emotion, these colors can be anything from vibrant, powerful, or exuberant to lively, youthful, or welcoming. It can capture attention and stimulate emotion, reflect comfort or even sterility." The firm takes into consideration an emotional point of view, leveraging color associations and resulting psychological effects.

At Chimera, the process of color selection is fairly systematic. Teasdale explains, "After detecting the core color, we either harness it as a standalone; combine it with its monochromatic breakdowns; or introduce a holding, achromatic, contrasting, clashing, or complementary color. It is often in the combination of colors that we create the perfect design combination. The power of color creates impact and drive, where the base color acts as a means to showcase its partner while adding depth and stability."

"We spend considerable time applying design themes before choosing the preferred options for final submission. The correct application and interpretation is critical in strengthening the core of any design." —Keelie Teasdale

aquacon2001

Aquacon is a conference and trade show for all sectors of the Australian aquatic industry. Though corporate, the identity and supporting material had to reflect aspects of sport and leisure. The identity itself was created to appear as if viewed through water. It has a slightly distorted perspective that implies constant movement and reflection. Color enhances this sense of movement through the use of analogous blues seen through each other. These cool colors, although refreshing and meditative in themselves, together create a whirlpool of youthful, effervescent energy.

Victoria's State Netball Hockey Centre is a premier sporting facility located in the heart of Melbourne's sporting district. As part of their branding, they requested three murals designed to support and extend the facility's new corporate identity. Carried from the identity through to the wall graphics, the three colors accompanied by white are distinctly Australian in feel and are used to represent the stadium's three key aspects: red for management, blue for netball, and green for hockey.

As high-chroma colors, they are clear, distinctive, and dynamic. The chosen colors allow white to stand proudly, lightening and opening up the design. Combined with linear graphics and bitmap photography, the colors intensify notions of movement, enthusiasm, and sporting passion.

Dynamo
Dublin, Ireland

Dynamo, established in 1992, is one of Ireland's most respected design consultancies, combining award-winning design with intuitive strategic thinking. Since its inception, the firm has developed expert creative skills to meet the diverse requirements of its varied client base. It has added new skills, new technologies, new people, and new thinking to evolve into a hybrid communications company. Dynamo does print and brand identity, motion graphics, interactive design, and packing for consumer brands.

Although it owned the lion's share of the Irish snack food market for some years, Tayto was losing ground to new market entrants such as Pringles and Walkers and feeling pressure from fragmentation in the snack food marketplace.

Dynamo's comprehensive rebranding pushes Mr. Tayto, the figurative mascot of the brand, to center stage. The character is redrawn and promoted to a role of quality endorser, creating cohesion and consistency throughout Tayto's varied product offerings. The new packaging also introduces a smile device to the color scheme and graphic elements that maximize the brand's accessibility and friendly personality. Designs for the packages predominantly feature the primary colors red, yellow, and blue. These colors work with a few accent hues to give the snack foods high-impact shelf appeal.

Consumer research at the time of relaunch reported both relief and excitement that the redesign had honored the favored snack brand while significantly improving the product's appearance and visibility. Tayto witnessed steady growth after the redesign, with market share increasing from 43 to 50 percent. Tayto marketing director PJ Brigdale says, "The new packaging design has created far-reaching potential for the Tayto brand, influencing a host of promotional opportunities we hadn't considered before." There is a bold simplicity in the Tayto packaging that is enhanced by high-visibility color palettes.

"We want to create communication programs that enhance brand performance. And we achieve consistent results by adopting an intuitive, strategic approach to brand communications. That means strategy borne out of common sense and instinct rather than a fixed restrictive process," says creative director Jamie Helly. As a result of this philosophy, Dynamo creates memorable and engaging work for a variety of industries and audiences.

Dynamo's use of color adds a new dimension to corporate communications and packaging. Its work in consumer products uses color in way that facilitates awareness and recall. Its bright, clear palettes evoke an emotional response, subliminal at times, that suggests the need for something new in a consumer's mind. Dynamo makes effective use of limited colors as well as full-color higher-budget projects. Color works especially hard in its designs to grab attention and keep it.

Honest is a new snack offering from Tayto. This product responds to consumer insights charting the trends toward more convenient, healthy offerings. Tayto went one better by creating a premium healthy snack, previously nonexistent in the Irish and UK snack markets. Dynamo eschewed the usual Technicolor approach to snack packaging, instead adopting a blanched color scheme. White is a not often seen in this hugely competitive food category, so its use lends significant visibility in a crowded store environment. The package's design takes on an editorial style that breaks rules and attracts discerning, health-conscious consumers.

As Yoplait's brand consultants, Dynamo was given the task of creating a new identity for the reformulated replacement for an ailing diet brand. Dynamo responded with a new brand name, Yoplait 0%, to maximize shelf presence. The labels are color-coded and utilize photos that correspond to product ingredients. This colorway system creates a delicious-looking range of products with clearly distinguished flavors, making consumer selection easy.

The Lucas Bols group is a subsidiary of Remy Cointreau SA, the global liqueur distillery. Bols approached Dynamo with an ambitious brief for creating a new brand identity for their innovative *Total Cocktail's* idea. The initiative is designed to provide advice, training, and supplier contacts for people interested in selling and serving alcoholic cocktails. The innovative offer allowed Bols to assume ownership of cocktail-making itself, enabling promotion of their wide range of cocktail mix liqueurs.

Dynamo's work for Bols includes a pocket-sized bartender's handbook and sales presentation materials. The design for Total Cocktails suggests the alchemy of drinks and ice. The visual style is reminiscent of 1950s cocktail lounges blended with contemporary typography.

The Bols *Total Cocktail's* booklet uses a palette of vivid colors to signpost the book's extensive index of cocktail recipes. Full-colored solid backgrounds are used throughout to bookmark popular cocktails by representing the drinks' ingredients. The Cosmopolitan, for example, is set against a bright pink. Color is used as punctuation in these pieces.

if it all seems like too much hard work

leave it to us - we've got the solution!

Running worldwide motivation and incentive programs
used to be an impossible challenge... but not any more!

At Globoforce, we've embraced the 'global village' to bring you motivation
solutions with global reach, and awards redeemable almost anywhere
in the world.

Like you, we recognize the importance of thinking on a global scale -
but equally the importance of being relevant, personable and local.

So we don't just talk the talk when it comes to 'thinking global'
and 'acting local'... we walk the walk too!

Interested? Collect your own $/€/£20 reward when you talk
to us at www.globoforce.com/makingcontact. We will contact
you to arrange a meeting and deliver your award which can
be redeemed at any one of thousands of merchants worldwide
– see for yourself just how motivating our rewards can be.

About Globoforce

Globoforce is the leading worldwide provider of employee, distribution
channel and consumer motivation solutions. Experts in providing end-to-
end solutions for motivational, loyalty, recognition, reward and incentive
programs for leading international companies. Currently covering 35
countries and growing fast, we design tailor-made motivation solutions
and incentive management systems, and of course, deliver the awards
themselves, whether its around the corner or around the world. Why not
drop us a line to say hello at corporate@globoforce.com or discover a
world of possibility at www.globoforce.com

globoforce

Globoforce offers an innovative incentive management system to large organizations intent on maximizing workforce productivity. Using leading-edge database development and Web technology, Globoforce designs, implements, and manages incentive and motivational programs for clients.

Dynamo created marketing campaigns, both print and online, that raise Globoforce's profile and help potential clients understand the firm's complex offerings. Clear hues, constructed around a palette of citrus colors, enliven the designs, making them appealingly accessible standouts among their competitors. Brightly colored transparent envelopes deliver direct mail offers and express Globofore's visible difference.

Fauxpas Grafik
Zurich, Switzerland

Fauxpas Grafik was founded in 2001 by partners Martin Stillhart and Giles Bachmann. Stillhart studied at the Schule für Gestaltung in Basel, Switzerland, while Bachmann studied at Höhere Schule für Gestaltung in Zürich. Together with a small staff, they are engaged in various areas of design. Fauxpas Grafik functions is an architectural office, book publisher, and cultural institution. The firm works primarily in print and sometimes in online design. Their work includes packaging, logos, direct mail, posters, books, and websites. In addition to commissioned work, Fauxpas Grafik sells its own products, including boxed sets of custom-designed rubber stamps.

Partner Giles Bachman sums up Fauxpas Grafik's design philosophy: "We are inspired by the possibilities or limitations of various production methods. We feel it is important to integrate the client into the design process." The result of this point of view is a breadth of work ranging from modern corporate to more experimental art styles.

Although Fauxpas Grafik professes no specific color philosophy, Bachman says, "Our print projects often use two colors. Adding a third color makes the piece stand on its own. Red and black are a frequently used combination, sometimes just as a starting point." The firm's work often contains massive blocks of limited colors, sometimes used for a bold graphic simplicity, at other times handled more subtly for an elegant, modern effect.

Ken is a Swiss-based architecture company. Ken is also a Japanese system of measurement. Fauxpas Grafik's designers were inspired by Japanese puzzles when they designed the logo for the architectural firm. The Ken identity features bits and pieces of black shapes rearranged and repositioned in various applications, such as the firm's website and poster, shown above.

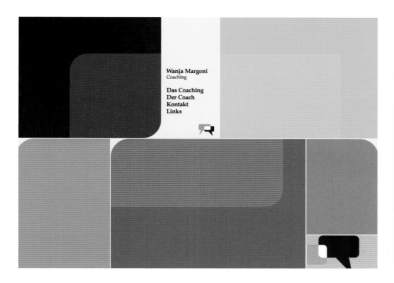

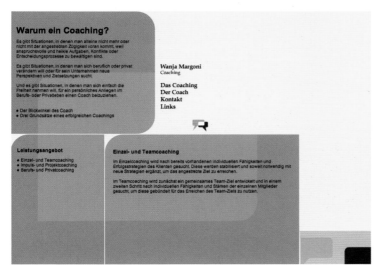

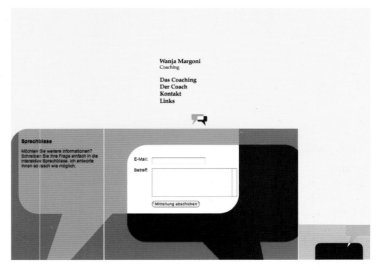

In this website for professional coach Wanja Margoni, the designers worked with a simple grid of ever-shifting colored shapes. The website shows Margoni's capabilities as well as his working process, featuring colored surfaces that are warm and inviting. Yellow ochre, deep olive green, and a burnished red represent Margoni's friendly approach.

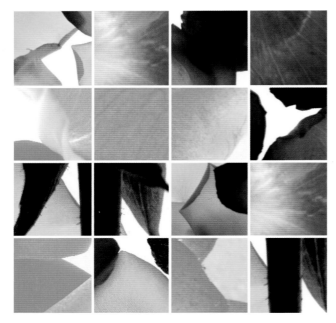

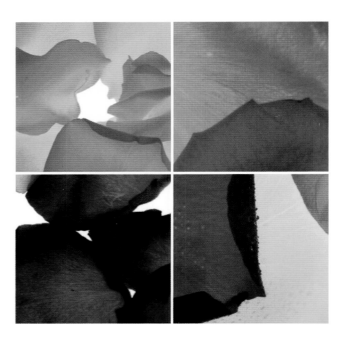

Rosengärten
Schulthess-Gartenpreis 2003

www.heimatschutz.ch
www.patrimoinesuisse.ch

SCHWEIZER HEIMATSCHUTZ
PATRIMOINE SUISSE
HEIMATSCHUTZ SVIZZERA
PROTECZIUN DA LA PATRIA

The Swiss Heritage Society commends exemplary achievement with the
Schulthess Horticultural Prize. Partner Martin Stillhart explains, "We tried
to put a modern face on an old-fashioned theme." The colors in this award
brochure come primarily from a series of photographs. The designers put rose
petals and leaves on a light table and photographed them. The backlighting
gives the flowers their special colored glow.

Color is used in an architectural manner for the Swiss Heritage Society. The Society also recognizes and commends exemplary achievement in architecture by awarding the Wakker Prize for the best-developed Swiss town. Fauxpas Grafik created a brochure, invitation, and poster (above) for this award. The poster is printed in serigraphic technique, with white circles overprinting black text passages on the cream-colored paper stock.

Green Dragon Office
Los Angeles, USA

The Green Dragon Office is led by its founder and creative director Lorraine Wild. As a designer, writer, critic, lecturer, and faculty member of the Program in Graphic Design at California Institute of the Arts (CalArts), Wild has been a highly influential figure to scores of students, teachers, practitioners, and thinkers in the field of graphic design. Her new venture, Green Dragon Office, is a collaborative studio that designs publications, identities, websites, posters, signage, and other communication media for clients ranging from museums to schools, publishers, corporations, and nonprofit organizations of all types.

The San Francisco Museum of Modern Art notes, "Lorraine Wild produces graphic designs that have the effortless grace of information that falls into place. She is a master of Modernism who champions sparse, abstract design disciplined by an invisible grid." As a designer, Wild is probably best known for books. Green Dragon Office continues to design books as well as broaden the scope of projects. Wild explains, "Underpinning our work is an obsession with direct collaboration with artists, architects, writers, editors, and curators. Our work is diverse because we strive to keep our process free of preconceptions. We try to create communication that reflects the intelligence and spirit of our collaborations, which are specific to each project. We translate those ideas into forms that audiences will remember and appreciate."

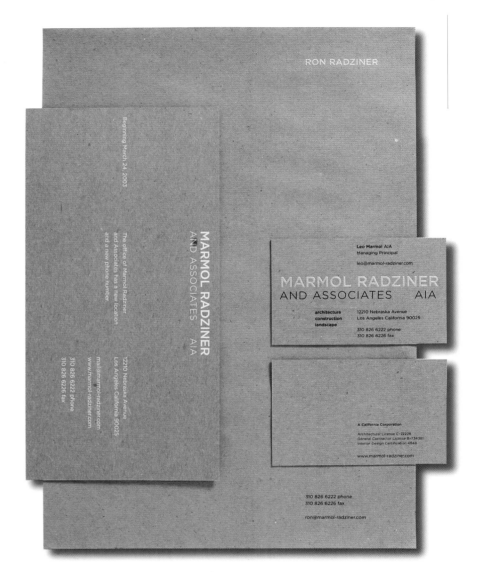

For the architectural firm Marmol Radziner and Associates, the designers represented the firm with a mix of slick high-end technology elements, such as high-tech type; silver inks; and earthy, crafty elements such as the textured stock.

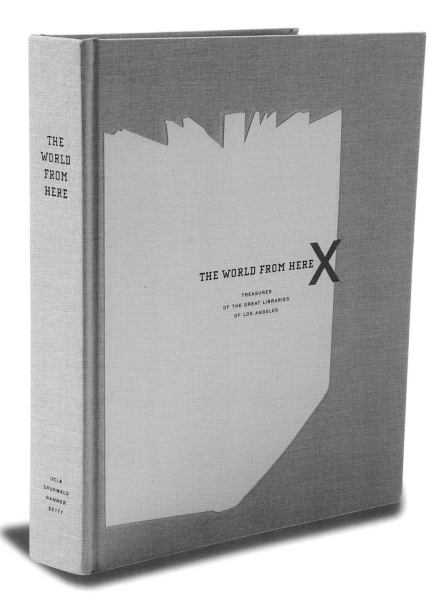

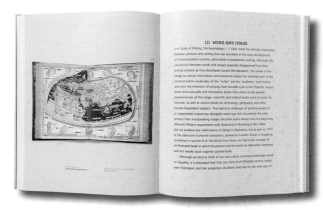

This book accompanies the exhibition The World from Here: Treasures of the Great Libraries of Los Angeles. The exhibition features a collection of rare books, letters, and manuscripts and encourages a deeper understanding of how these important artifacts represent the history of ideas.

For the book design, Lorraine Wild breaks the large volume into sections. Each section is dominated by a desaturated tint. Journeying through the material, the neighboring section shifts to the next hue positioned on the color wheel. The designers use book silhouettes both on the cover, above left, and throughout as a unifying element.

Lorraine Wild says about her philosophy of color usage, "Color can go beyond decoration and instead can be used as a structural element that helps organize the page. A good example is the shifting color backgrounds in *The World from Here* book [pictured on page 165] or the use of dark brown to indicate archival material in Mike Kelly's *The Uncanny* [opposite page]. Those [color] decisions are driven not by aesthetics but from a need to communicate something about the content of the book."

Color is used as part of a set of design elements that often includes diverse typefaces, disparate layouts, unusual images, and dense bodies of text. Together these elements can form logical and beautiful relationships in service to content and meaning. When asked about using a recognizable color palette in the work, Wild responds, "We stay away from primary colors, except for the occasional blast of PMS warm red on a book design. I'm interested in more complex color relationships than the high-contrast effects associated with primaries."

These philosophical approaches seem to be working. Wild's designs are responsive and stand out for their subtlety in a communications-saturated world. Designer Laurie Haycock Makela, a former CalArts colleague, summarizes, "I admire her work because it speaks for many cultural institutions of our time in alternating fits of elegance and anarchy."

"We know intuitively that our personal struggle with idealism and pragmatism is affected by the values we bring to our work and the context in which we create it."
—Lorraine Wild

The cover of a book about artist Florine Stettheimer's *Manhattan Fantastica* series of paintings and drawings was the first time Wild was able to allude to an artist's work rather than simply display a piece of art. The designer used hot pink printed on the book cover and an orange-colored doily pattern printed on a translucent overlay dust jacket to achieve a strange color effect not typical of offset printing. The play of the transparency and the saturated cover color resulting from the layering creates a distinctive color interaction.

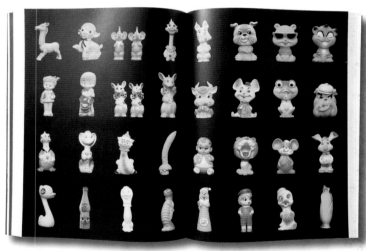

The Uncanny, by Mike Kelly, is the restaging of an exhibition in the 1990s and the second version of this book. The essay from the first book is reprinted here with a brown frame and brown type (upper right). The images from the first book are reprinted in fake sepia (lower left), while new images are printed in color (upper left and lower right). The effect is an organic unity holding the odd collection together.

Johnson banks
London, UK

Johnson banks provides creative and pragmatic solutions to communications problems in a smart and lively way. Its interpretations produce designs that keep clients' brands fresh and in the public consciousness. Looking at the firm's work gives a sense that there is thinking behind the graphics.

What might be especially unexpected in the work of Johnson banks is its use of color. If designers are influenced by the region of the world in which they live, then creative director Michael Johnson's color palettes are not what should be, given the grayness of London. His work typically features pure vivid colors, often jewel toned. The brightness of his choices make color a powerful tool in causing the firm's work to stand out in cluttered environments, both physical and printed.

Johnson banks uses color purposefully. There is a sense of clear color harmonies and unusual associations, such as the integration of sound and color, as used in the Science Museum wayfinding system shown on page 168.

For one of the preeminent British design companies, Johnson banks has a very un-stereotypically British notion of color. Perhaps it is because Johnson has worked around the world, incorporating the influences of Sydney, Melbourne, Tokyo, and New York, as well as the worlds of advertising and design into his work.

"There exist some great opportunities in the design industry." —**Michael Johnson**

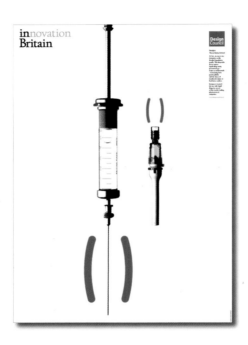

The British Design Council wanted a set of posters featuring some of the 1,000-odd products that were part of its Millennium Products campaign. The only problem was that these posters were for a worldwide, not-always-English-speaking audience. By using pictures and symbols, Johnson banks created a visual language that any person of any culture could probably read, or at least decode. The minimally colored posters—Intraject, a syringe without a needle (left), and the Nautilus loudspeakers, the name inspired by its shell namesake (right)—feature stark white backgrounds with silhouettes of the products This highlights the imagery, providing a focused experience for the viewer.

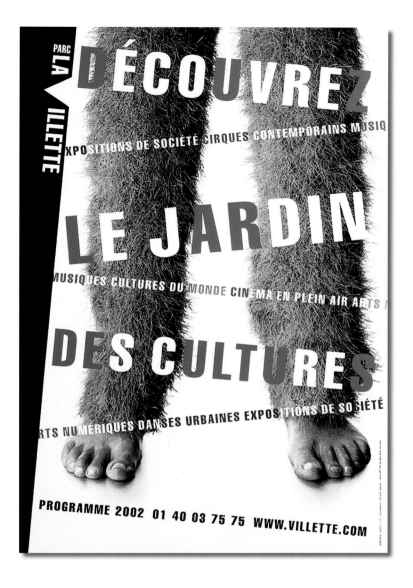

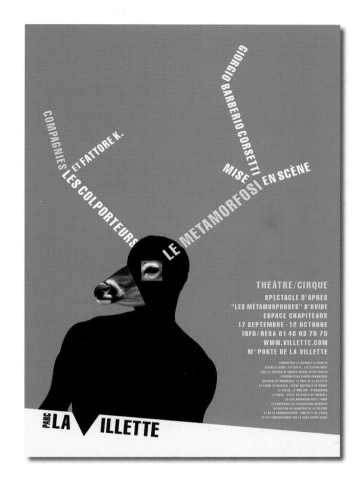

"How do you evolve a favorite French cultural institution? Let them own the edges of everything they do," is how Johnson banks describes the problem and solution for the Parc de la Villette. The client needed a link to the old identity, but let them present everything as clearly coming from the Parc. There was no point in designing a traditional symbol for the client—they needed something more substantial. Johnson banks proposed a new identity device—a black border graphic running along the edge of every piece of print the client develops. The designers also imposed limitations: one weight of one typeface and a single, powerful image. The two

applications (above) show this edge identity in action. "*Découvrez le jardin des cultures*" (*Discover the garden of cultures*), at left, is a promotion for the Parc. "Our thought was to take the grass of the park and use it to make iconic images, so grass becomes a linking idea," says Johnson. The Métamorphoses Poster (right) is for a theater event at the Parc. It features a silhouette of a man with a photo of a deer's eye and muzzle superimposed, and typography forming the antlers, illustrating metamorphosis. The pure, bold blue attracts the eye and speaks of clear blue skies.

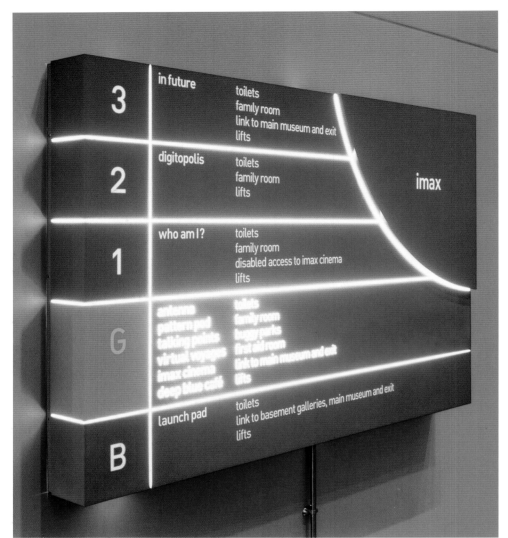

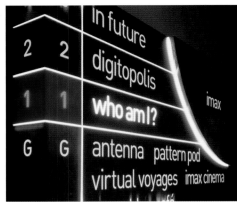

The new Welcome Wing extension to the Science Museum in London overwhelms the senses with its vast, dark, cathedral-like space. The space is crammed to the gills with state-of-the-art examples of twenty-first century science and technology, so the client needed a way to stop visitors from wandering around the wing like lost sheep and help them locate the things they wanted to see.

Johnson banks developed a set of self-illuminating beacons (above) with pulsing letters and embedded sound chips, each with its own note, playing the music of the wing.

Whether standing on the third floor platform or in an entrance, visitors can work out where they are by a combination of color and sound. These wayfinding graphics utilize a series of jewel-toned colors against black backgrounds, mirroring the exhibition space itself and providing easy-to-read signage.

With the darkened corridors of the wing, another level of signage (above) was required, one that dealt with the nitty-gritty of getting from elevators to exhibitions, or deciding which way to go from decision points on stairs. The suite of self-illuminated signs is based on a cross section of the wing and further helps visitors navigate through the space.

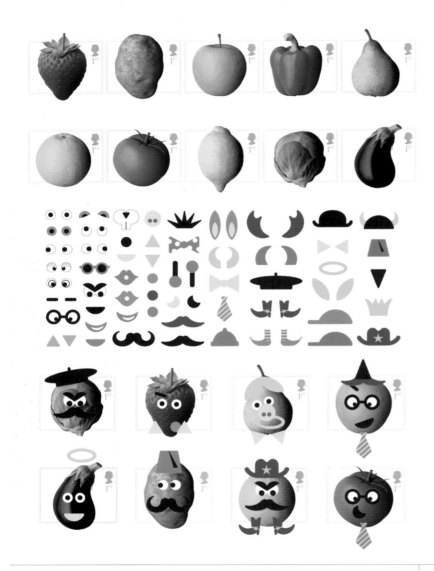

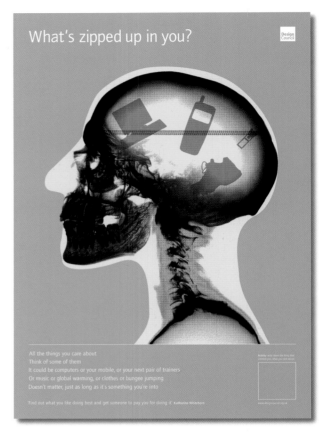

The Fruit and Veg stamps for the UK's Royal Mail are strikingly original. The stamp kit contains ten stamps with illustrations of fruits and vegetables rendered in a classical realistic style, accompanied by seventy-six stickers of facial features and accessories that allow postal customers to produce their own personalized stamps. The brief was to create interactive stamps for children. The designers where inspired by the kids' game Mr. Potato Head. This fun piece again showcases the firm's preference for bright color palettes—the perfect recipe for an audience of children.

The "What's zipped up in you?" classroom card for the British Design Council is one in a series that johnson banks created to encourage students to take part in a design workshop. The vivid colors, especially the lime and fuchsia utilized as backgrounds, were chosen to brighten up dingy British classrooms and to invite young people to think about things in their world that they would like to redesign.

slow   slower   slowest

Comparative superlative

BRITISH COUNCIL

drink   drank   drunk

Irregular verbs

BRITISH COUNCIL

or   ?

UK or USA

BRITISH COUNCIL

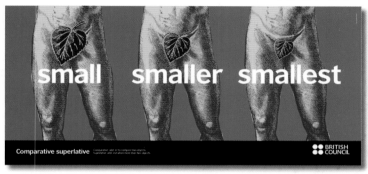

small   smaller smallest

Comparative superlative

BRITISH COUNCIL

a sore saw

Homophones

BRITISH COUNCIL

write

Silent letters

BRITISH COUNCIL

Making learning English fun, not exhausting, was the goal of this project. The 900-odd classrooms worldwide that the British Council uses to teach English are not the most inspiring of places. Combine that with a heavy session of conjunctive-auxiliary-phrasal-pronouns, and Johnson banks could see legions of keen young students falling into deep comas at their desks. After poring over English grammar books, the designers created forty classroom cards.

Uwe Loesch
Erkath, Germany

Uwe Loesch is an internationally recognized poster designer (*Plakatgestalter*) and professor at the Bergi University of Wuppertal in Düsseldorf. Although Professor Loesch works in a variety of media, including book and catalog design, identity establishment, and campaigns for social and cultural institutions, he is known best for his posters.

Loesch's posters have strong meanings and messages delivered with a minimalist approach. He does not have a predefined visual style. He works with intelligence, wit, strong contrast, and the interaction of words and images to raise awareness for a variety of sociopolitical causes. Growing up in postwar Germany affected the way Loesch perceives and transmits ideas. He adopted the poster early in his career as his medium for bringing about change.

Loesch's work philosophy is "I see more or less, never the less!" and he admits to being influenced by the nihilistic French art movement Dada. In response to our consumerism-saturated world, Loesch has said, "Wait a minute. If everyone keeps shouting louder and louder, no one will be able to hear, much less understand or believe, anything." As a result of this point of view, his work tends to whisper and actively engage the viewer in drawing conclusions. Whispering often results in restrained, clever typography and color usage.

This poster, called *Game Over* (*...und raus bist du*) (translates to "...and you are out," referring to eliminating someone from a child's game) was created for the competition Children Are the Rhythm of the World, organized by the Deutsches Plakatmuseum Essen. The poster features the portrait of a young African soldier that has been color manipulated to take on the character of military camouflage. The blood-red typography—the subject of which is a German children's rhyme about the game hide-and-seek—overlays the image.

For EBV-scan Düsseldorf, a lithography company, Loesch created this poster to invite customers to a party for presenting new scanner technology imported from Japan. Loesch calls this poster *Squaring the Circle Is an Art Itself,* and the central image is a parody of the Japanese flag. The designer has squared the flag's red circle, placing it on a white field with spare typography.

In this poster for the Cultural Festival of North-Rhine Westphalia, the torn pieces of white paper are a kind of social sculpture symbolizing the difficulties in bringing cultures together. The poster is called *I Could Be Nice: Tolerance of Cultures—Culture of Tolerance.* The colors are black, white, and red, the typical colors of political posters in the twentieth century.

"Generally, I use color in my work very purposefully."
—Uwe Loesch

Loesch uses color sparingly. He notes, "Color decorates, color irritates, color seduces, color makes you blind. Therefore, I prefer black on white." Loesch scrutinizes color photography images and determines whether they work in order to "celebrate the difference between the nature-beautiful and the art-beautiful."

Red is the color most present in Loesch's work. He believes it is the best auxiliary color to black-and-white, adding, "Red is synonymous with poster." Loesch occasionally uses fluorescent colors that he thinks are particularly suitable for signaling, and other color schemes if they are specific to the message and culture he is working with. However, because red is a symbol of a number of messages, he uses it often.

Loesch feels that color plays a crucial role in the communication process. "In the sequence of perception, color is noticed before the form. To see red without thinking red is not possible, at least in the Western world," says Loesch.

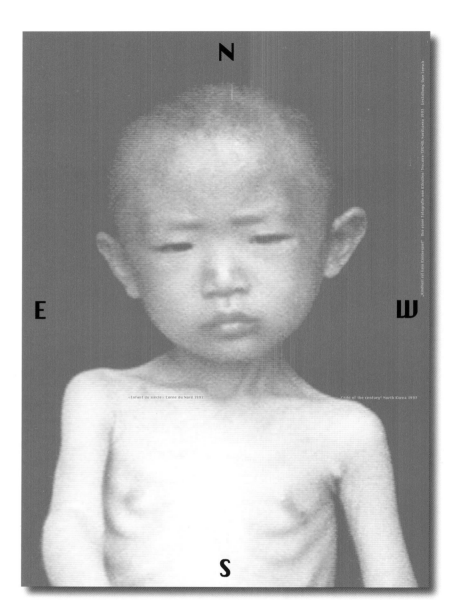

This poster was created for the exhibition Childhood Is Not a Children's Play, organized by the Deutsches Plakatmuseum Essen. Loesch calls this poster *Child of the Century.* It features the saturated image of a small starving child from North Korea. The designer uses red symbolically throughout his work to draw attention to social causes.

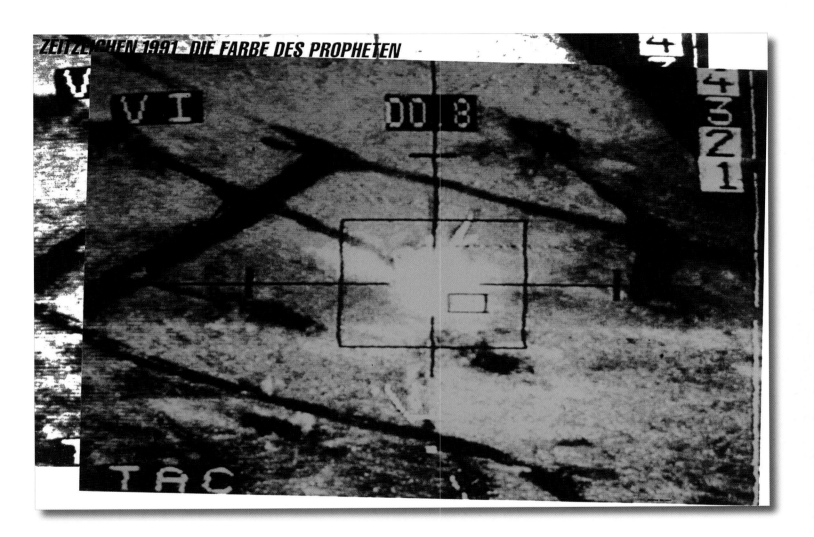

This poster was created in 1991 during the first Gulf War. The designer uses the double exposure of repeating images taken from satellite weaponry gun sites. The desaturated blue over the black-and-white image simulates night and conveys a sense of foreboding. It is an example of what has been referred to as Loesch's "strategy of irritation," in which he deliberately causes a shift in perception by using very small changes in the expected presentation of his graphic elements.

Lorenc + Yoo Design
Atlanta, USA

Lorenc + Yoo Design is an Atlanta-based environmental graphic design firm whose projects include retail spaces, tradeshow exhibits, furniture design, wayfinding signage, museum exhibitions, and event and corporate visitor center environmental graphics. Partners Jan Lorenc and Chung Youl Yoo came from very different cultural backgrounds. Lorenc emigrated to the United States from Poland as a boy, while Yoo immigrated more recently from Korea via Paraguay. Together they work within a wide range of stylistic environments and vocabularies for a variety of clients.

Lorenc + Yoo Design's philosophy is one of exploration, inquisitiveness, and commitment to innovation. Its approach centers on collaboration among design disciplines, allowing each client's persona to come through in the executed design. Lorenc + Yoo Design teams include architects; interior, industrial, and graphic designers; and a cadre of specific consultants assembled to meet the needs of a given project. They share ideas, ask questions, and engage in constructive criticism among the disciplines in order to achieve an integrated design solution.

Both Lorenc and Yoo believe in design as narration; they tell client and brand stories through the environments that they create. The designers use color as an important element in their storytelling. Partner Jan Lorenc explains, "The color needs to narrate the focus of the space. Your journey through the space can be packaged by pieces of content wrapped in a focal color that evolves with the content." To keep the experience fresh and interesting, the designers tend to use color judiciously. Lorenc continues, "If one uses the entire color palette within all parts of the space, it doesn't work. It gets tiring. There needs to be a reason behind the use of color."

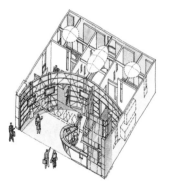

The Palladium Company develops urban centers that are prime destinations for shopping, residences, and entertainment. This is its exhibit for industry conventions. Finishes, materials, and colors are all inspired by Palladium's development and construction styles. The exhibit is a modern classic, dominated by blues and silvers, which are frequently used in Palladium's architecture.

Haworth, one of the largest and most respected furniture manufacturers in the United States, asked Lorenc + Yoo Design to redesign its existing showroom spaces. The company wanted its spaces to complement product display and establish a bold identity expressing its vision, core values, and key "stories." The result is a visually dynamic environment that communicates on a variety of levels while solving pragmatic constraints.

A bold color palette of apple green and sky blue combined with black-and- white graphics, metaphorical images, and witty copy were employed to communicate Haworth's multifaceted nature. Color was applied in an architectonic manner, creating focal elements in the space, as well as dematerializing a forest of internal structural columns to form an artistic graphic composition.

"The message of "calm," "energetic," "loud," and so on can be complemented and communicated by the use of color in a spatial strategy."
—Jan Lorenc

In environments, many spaces may be visible simultaneously, so the design can be seen in one overall glance. Thus the use of color becomes an organizing or thematic medium in Lorenc + Yoo Design's work. In addition, the designers look for equity their clients may have in a particular color scheme and incorporate that into the overall strategy. In exhibits, color is tied more directly to corporate identity and brand messaging, but it is used in a subtle way with punctuations of punchy color. For their work in signage, which tends to have greater longevity in terms of display usage, color and materials are tied to the interior design or the architecture of the building.

The firm has no set color palette, although the principals admit to using a lot of silver-colored metals, such as aluminum and stainless steel. Jan Lorenc describes color selections as "totally dependent on the intent of the project." He says, "We learn about the effects and intensities of colors to see what the space is like and build a digital or physical walk-through model. The physical model is the best way to see the space, since you can walk through it in your own mind at your own pace without the technology hindering your participation." Either way, the designers visualize the spatial sensation of their color choices before implementation.

Designed to stand in stark contrast to the visually hyperactive booths nearby, the Sony Ericsson Exhibit spells out the two capital letters of the newly formed company it represents (see opposite page). Simultaneously weighty and massive yet ethereal and fluid, the undulating planes of the *S* and *E* letterforms symbolize both the client's prominent positions of strength and its futuristic outlook.

The two-level structure accommodates the dual nature of the exhibit. Product demonstration and reception areas are on the first floor, and private conference space is on the second. Once inside the space, visitors occupy a surreal environment of technology, focused on previewing small electronic devices. The exhibit has a landmark quality and is a place within a place that boldly communicates the client's vision.

Sony Ericsson products speak to young adults. The exhibit's interior finishes and displays are intended to appeal to this market through style, color, and overall ambience. The color palette is simple and direct for bold visual impact. Though the display is predominantly white, accent colors echo the client's new identity.

LUST
The Hague, Netherlands

LUST is a design, typography, and propaganda collaborative based in The Hague that was started in 1996 by Thomas Castro and Jeroen Barendse. The studio accepts commissioned work—such as books, posters, websites, and interactive projects for architects, art groups, designers, and publisers—and also produces self-initiated work, including type design. LUST describes its work as "typography graphic design abstract cartography mapping random mistake-ism fonts type design multimedia interactive Web design internet www art abstract big bang chaos."

Underpinning its work is a point of view that becomes apparent when understanding how LUST defines the concept behind the name of its company. LUST is "coincidence and coincidentalism, the exaltation of the insignificant, the degradation of form and content to its essence, magnification, and contextuality versus textuality." The designers do concede, however, "No one interpretation of LUST is correct. Your conclusion is just as valid as ours. LUST is, after all, personal."

For LUST, color is never a given or a must. It is another tool to use (or exploit) to communicate ideas. The designers use color to lend meaning to data visualization. Castro explains, "Because of our work methodology, there comes a point after the research phase where we are analyzing the data we have to design. At this stage, many analysis methods we use involve graphs, charts, tables, and matrices, so colors are used to define certain elements (e.g., categories, chronology, and subsets) of the data to be able to understand them and how they fit with each other." Many of these charts become an integral part of LUST's design solutions.

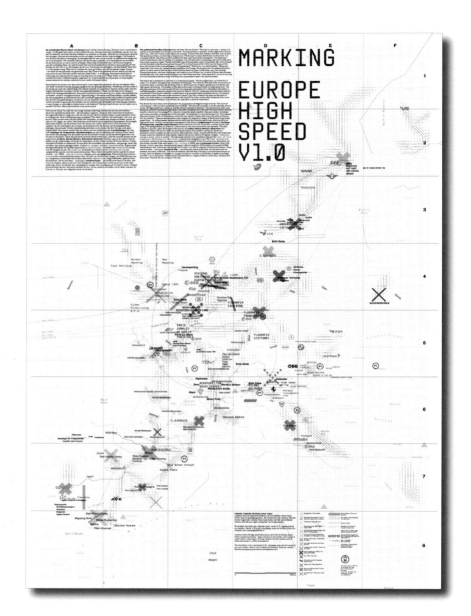

This map, made for Atelier HSL, is one of a series designed to spark passenger interest in traveling by Holland's high-speed train. Each map was released in sequence, leading up to a final digital atlas that will be featured in the trains themselves. This first map addresses the idea that traveling is not only going from point A to B by crossing several intersections, highlighting interesting places the train passes that could be points of departure for passengers' adventures.

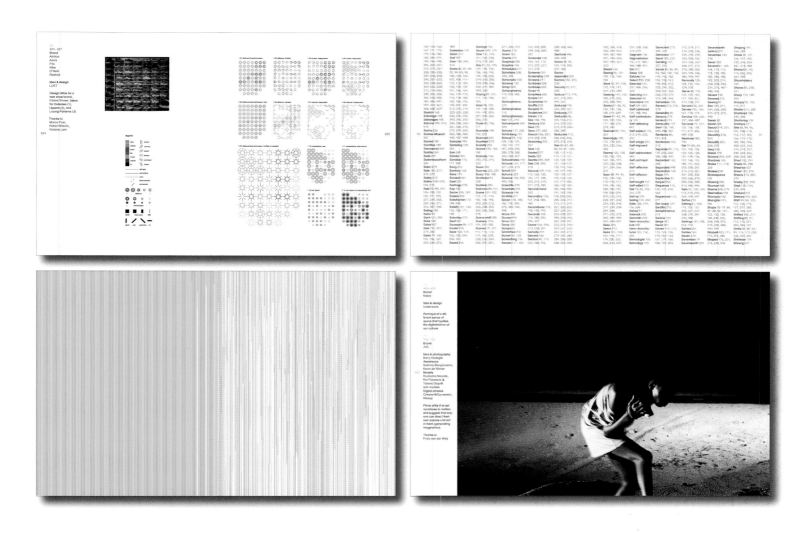

The map presents a few travel stories in a short text written in both Dutch and English. Places mentioned in the text are tagged on the maps. The copy invites the public to consider their own stories of the places and people they are visiting by train, thereby conceptually marking the map for themselves. A series of subdued yet highly transparent colors were used to represent the Xs and other markings to avoid cluttering the minute dots of the grid and flow lines of the rails. Silver was used for the grid and flow lines to add richness and depth.

Margeting: Inventing a Different Marketing Language is a book with a fresh approach to marketing by focusing on how consumers participate in the process. A recurrent theme is the use of rhizome (or nonhierarchy) as a marketing approach. The designers use this concept too. It is apparent in the book structure and page layouts. For example, nonhierarchy is employed by the use of only one font in one size and weight, so text importance is not imposed. Two types of color are used: fluorescent navigational elements, and dark hues for italicized information, helping the reader move through various levels of content.

"When color is approached conceptually instead of aesthetically, then it is often simply implemented in an easy and painless manner instead of forced or contrived."
—Thomas Castro

Color is an extension of the designers' analytical methods and is aesthetically pleasing as well. Elements such as columns of text or indices are colorful expressions of meaning and context. Colored grids add visual richness but also define a relative scale.

LUST's color palettes are always derived from what is being communicated and the medium used for communication. Castro says, "In our mapping work, it is important to have colors that are easily distinguished. Also, we tend to use colors that are based on 100-percent coverage of one or more of the CMYK colors." This choice is due to legibility and vibrancy of color. "For projects related to the screen," Castro continues, "colors are chosen for different reasons: saturation, color vibration, color temperature, glare, overscan, etc. These all relate." The designers have also experimented with randomly generated color, especially in their recent website work, but Thomas Castro states, "It is never an indiscriminate choice, even if the colors are generated randomly."

This series of three maps was designed to provide a self-guided tour of special projects built in the *Vinex* (government-developed communities of The Hague) for the celebration of the Day of Architecture in Holland. A colorful matrix navigation system designed as an index of projects by location and architect is the dominant visual identity. Color is bright to stand out in a background of typography. The designers chose not to use typical geographic color notations (e.g., blue outlines for lakes) and instead used gray outlines to represent geographic features, in order to let the color representing architectural projects stand out. The result is a fresh, contemporary take on mapping. (Interiors not shown.)

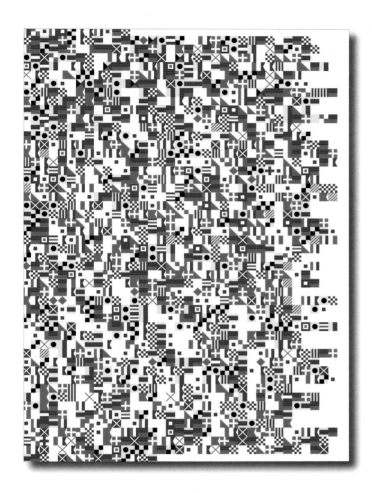

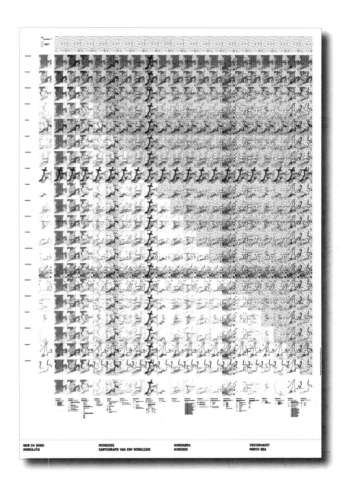

LUST self-published this project, which stems from the research the designers did for a mapping project of Hoek van Holland (an area of Rotterdam bordering on the North Sea). There was much unused research, so the designers created *Noord Zee: Cartografie van eeen wereld zee* (*North Sea: Cartography of a World Sea*), an atlas of twenty topical maps that tie together historical, cultural, and geographical information in an interesting way. Essentially, this project investigates what could be called North Sea culture. The maps offer a range of information on the area's fishing, religions, ethnicity, shipwrecks, and more. Here again, transparent rich color adds to navigational ease, improved legibility, and visual texture. The content of the maps tends to be highly conceptual visual representations of information in which data become colorful graphic patterns.

A detail of these Noord Zee maps can be seen on pages 186–187.

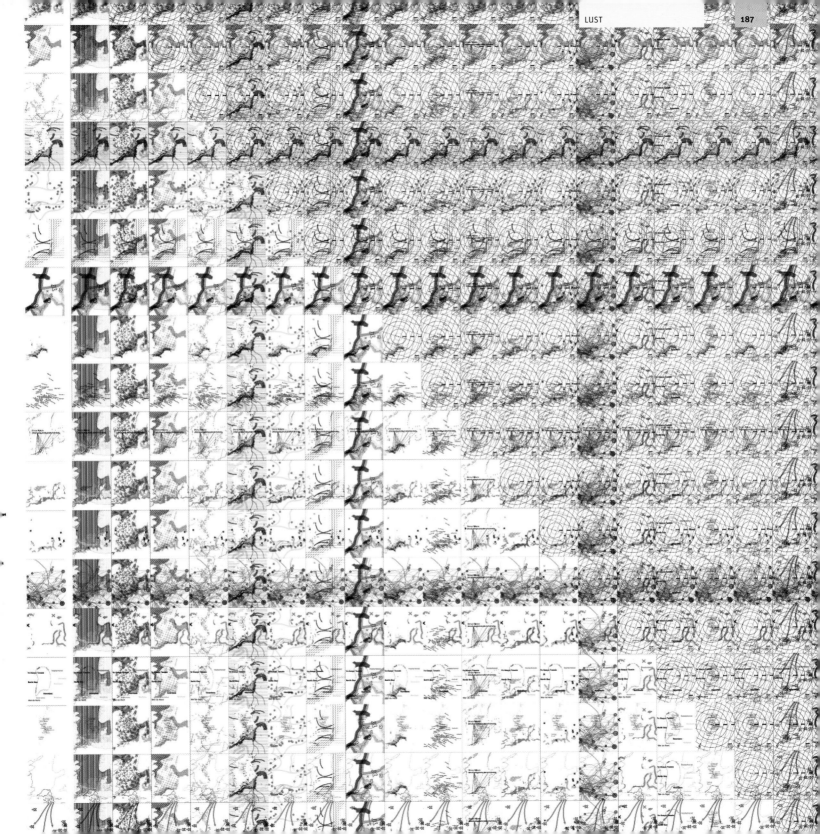

Methodologie, Inc.
Seattle, USA

Methodologie is a brand firm that specializes in comprehensive, business-critical communications systems such as brand development, investor communications, corporate identity systems, and print and interaction design. The firm's work is mostly business to business, with a strong presence in the "yin" industries, such as technology, biotech, and property development, balanced by the "yang" of nonprofit, human services, and fine arts clients. The designers say, "The hard side and soft side of our client list influence each other for the better."

Methodologie is very much a collaborative team of twenty members, with five principals and two creative directors, probably best known for their annual report projects. However, the firm's branding and Web practices are full-fledged offerings that continue the tradition of blending great strategy with beautiful design in corporate communications.

Of color philosophy, Methodologie says, "Colors are very slippery. They are part science, part art, part intuition, part business. As soon as we try to make a pure science out of it—which some studies prove is possible—we find we overthink it." The designers' approach to color selection depends on the project and the client, of course, but also on the context. "For an identity system where color plays a vital role and acts as a root system of the brand design, the colors need to be long lasting. In this case, we approach the selection of color deliberately and go through many rounds of color studies and revisions. We look at the client's competitive landscape to see how to stand out colorwise. The goal is really to own a color in a given category because it is unique but also because it so perfectly fits the brand," explains Methodologie.

Safeco, a top U.S. insurance company, offers an annual agent incentive program, the prize being a luxury trip in which top agents can attend seminars and relax with their spouses and colleagues. The island of Kauai was the destination for this year's program. The brochure (above) shows off the romantic side of Hawaii with a dreamy watercolor palette of light sky blues and sea greens. The overlapping translucency of the stock heightens the watery effect.

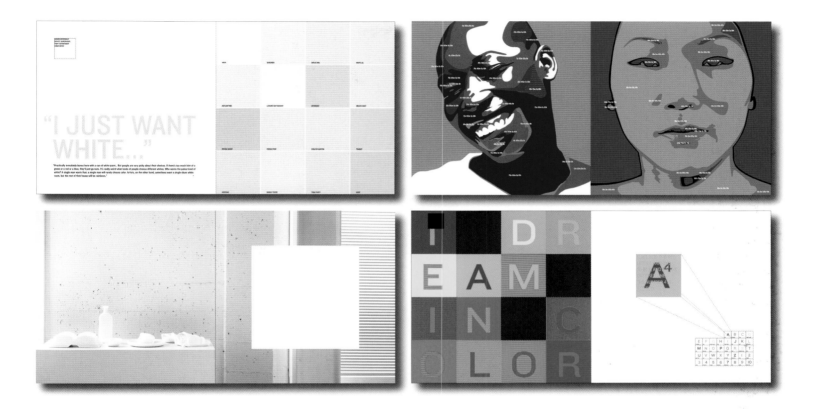

This is an image piece for the top West Coast commercial printer in the United States, Colorgraphics. The brochure, called "Speaking in Color," shows off the client's high-end printing capabilities and utilizes the theme of color. Methodologie developed the idea of asking people what color means to them. The designers interviewed groups of people about the role that color plays in their lives and then used these rich stories and thoughts verbatim, bringing them to life. The quotes and stories drive the color system and illustrate the colors people talk about. However, the cover, introduction, and supporting text throughout the book are white and gray to be as neutral as possible in order to let the color stories take center stage.

"Color is very emotional and subjective. No matter how much you try to objectify color, it remains personal."
—Dale Hart, **Methodolgie Creative Director**

For its annual report (AR) practice, Methodologie uses color in a flexible and fluid way because of the shorter lifespan of these projects. "There are two paths in the road of color for ARs. If the annual is driven strictly by the corporate brand, then the color palette will most often be derived directly from the specific brand colors. The other option is for color to be driven by the story of the annual that year," explains Methodologie. "On the Web, it's a whole different story. Colors that work great in print don't always have the same effect digitally. And you have so little control over what the user's monitor settings are that, to some extent, you have to give yourself over to it."

Methodologie realizes that color palettes shift with the fashion tides and tries to "just keep that spinning wheel of color fortune in the back of our minds." The firm tends to think that it has no specific kind of color palette. Rather, Methodologie says, "We try to design for our clients, not ourselves. One of the roles of our creative director is to keep an eye on Methodologie trends, just to ensure that a color is being chosen because it is appropriate, not because it is top of mind and handy."

Da Vinci Gourmet makes flavored syrups and sauces, typically used in espresso drinks by coffee house baristas the world over. Methodologie reinvented the company's identity and packaging to differentiate better among the items in the Da Vinci product line. The designers took a sophisticated, contemporary design approach by using translucent labels with solid white type that let the different syrups show through. Color appears only in the name of the flavor.

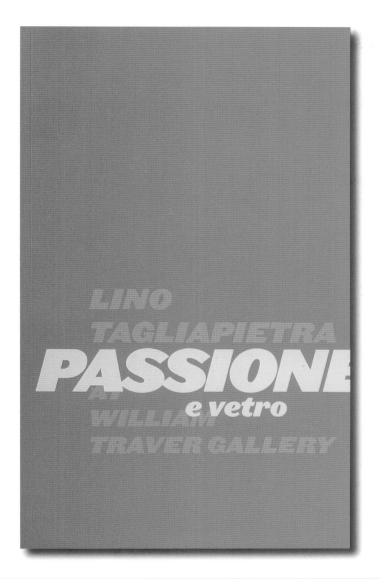

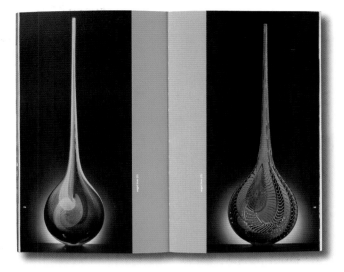

The William Traver Gallery's catalog for an exhibition of Italian glass art master Lino Tagliapietra is a dramatic high-end piece. The design was driven by the artist's one-of-a-kind wonders of vibrant color and gravity-defying forms. The designers photographed the artworks in pristine isolation and then highlighted each piece with a band of color next to the photo. The rich color palette was sampled from the artwork photos so each color would complement or contrast the art perfectly. Methodologie chose a bright fuchsia cover and hot yellow and pink for the typography so there would be no question that the catalog and Lino's work are a passionate celebration of color.

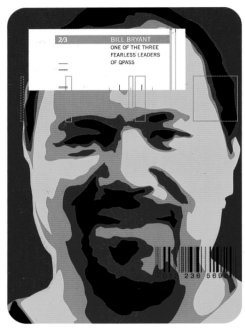

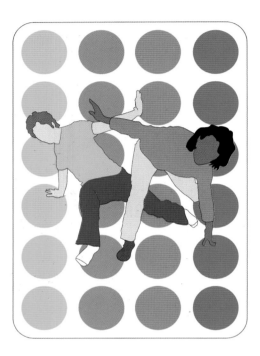

Qpass, a high-tech software company, wanted to relaunch its brand internally. The goal was to educate employees about the brand as the company switched its business to focus strictly on business-to-business markets. Qpass also wanted to get its staff excited about this switch. Methodologie developed an unorthodox campaign that centered on a unique brand card game and was supported by promotional items and a temporary redesign of Qpass's employee intranet site.

The spirit of the game and its wild and crazy design palette was a great fit for the break-the-rules culture of the young company. Each of thirty cards represented a brand element (mission, promise, among others), company fact (year founded, company folklore), or company association (primary market info, icon, among others). Each employee received ten random brand cards and was required to trade with other staffers to collect suits of like cards to win prizes.

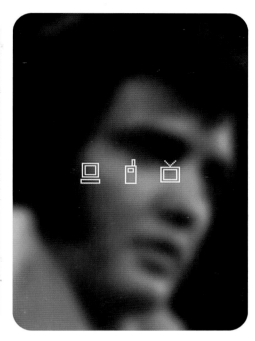

The color system was deliberately all over the map. The designers used it as playfully and satirically as possible. Methodologie marketing manager John Carroll says, "The whole system is really a carnival of color, no two cards being the same. We did this to make the game as 'uncorporate' as possible to appeal to the young, high-tech staff."

In addition to the cards, Methodologie created icons to represent aspects of the Qpass brand statement that were put on T-shirts (above right) in a mix of brand colors. In addition, five skins, or interface designs, that rotated usage were developed for the company's intranet site. Every time an employee logged on, he or she saw a variety of colorful patterns that promoted the Qpass brand game.

Morla Design
San Francisco, USA

Morla Design has an eclectic body of work ranging from identity to environments to books. One element that unifies the work is an adventurous use of color. Creative director Jennifer Morla takes risks with color within the context of appropriateness for her clients and their target audiences. "Oftentimes they say that design is a seductive propaganda, but it's not always trying to pull the wool over somebody's eyes. Design has to excite, but it has to inform in a way that engages. I try to involve the audience in the design process, whether they know it or not." She succeeds in this goal, often aided by her use of color.

According to Morla, "Extremes work. Really large, or really thick, or really small, or really colorful, or really simple, or really dense." Morla's typical approach to color is to choose a palette of about five base colors that best represent the ideas being conveyed in the project. She then picks two lighter colors that might be transparent in order to over-print the base colors. To round out the palette, she selects two additional colors that are denser and perhaps darker than the base colors to use as contrast and provide the ability to reverse colors out of them. This approach has been an effective way to build color systems.

As Morla said in a recent keynote speech to designers, "Passion enables us to remain true to our creative vision. Analyze, synthesize, visualize, but don't compromise."

"Design does not live in an aesthetic vacuum. Design is influenced by and influences contemporary society."
—Jennifer Morla

This is a pair of Levi's jeans... illustrates the past 140 years of Levi's 501 Jeans with more than 300 pages of people, places, and marketing that turned one brand into an American icon. The piece features eclectic typography, including vintage lettering, as well as western and historical imagery. The book has pull-out spreads, that add to its visual interest. Morla Design handled all aspects of production, from concept to delivery of 40,000 books. This piece is in the permanent collection of the San Francisco Museum of Modern Art.

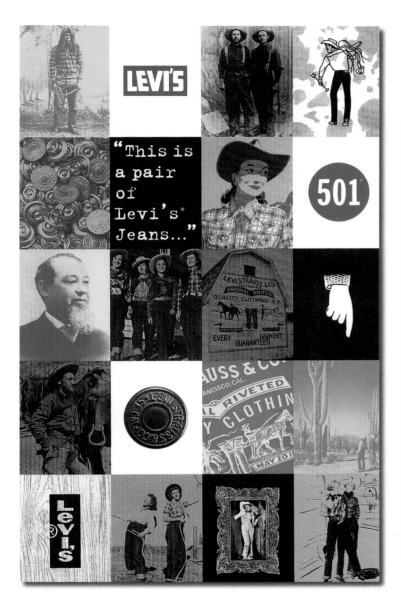

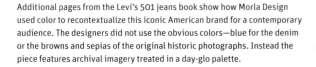

Additional pages from the Levi's 501 jeans book show how Morla Design used color to recontextualize this iconic American brand for a contemporary audience. The designers did not use the obvious colors—blue for the denim or the browns and sepias of the original historic photographs. Instead the piece features archival imagery treated in a day-glo palette.

The choice of high-key colors is also reference to the San Francisco of the 1960s—when Levi's became a big brand. These images are posterized and translated into two colors, often using complementary pairs.

For the Discovery Channel, Morla Design created a total brand identity and packaging system for implementation throughout the company's retail stores. The project encompassed shopping bags, gift boxes, and product packaging. Surface graphics include geometric spiral illustrations that layer and move to create moirélike patterns and reinforce the theme of discovery. Silk-screened, day-glo colors were used to attract young audiences, typically boys, and stand out in the stores' frenetic shopping mall locations.

United Airlines contacted Morla Design to create the cover art for its magazine *Hemispheres*. Neomodern in feel, the design is a playful combination of ellipses and circles. *Hemispheres* has won more awards than any other in-flight magazine in the United States, and 500,000 copies are read by 2 million people on United flights all over the globe each month. This piece was the first cover of the magazine after the September 11th tragedy, and Morla chose an upbeat color palette, using bright pastels. The design evokes a futuristic feeling that helped ease tensions and allowed passengers to relax and enjoy their flight.

The Mexican Museum twentieth anniversary poster commemorates the museum's collection of pre-Columbian, colonial, and contemporary Mexican art. The large benday portrait of famed painter Frida Kahlo and the quintessential image of Our Lady of Guadalupe combined with Lotteria game card imagery and ninetheenth-century Mexican wood-block type celebrate the varied heritage of Mexican arts and crafts. This contemporary presentation of classic imagery helps alter the perception that the museum houses strictly a pre-Columbian collection, while the vibrant colors are truly evocative of a Mexican marketplace.

The Bay Area Sports Organizing Committee chose Morla Design to create a poster to publicize San Francisco as the U.S. bid city for the Summer 2012 Olympic Games. The designers chose not to create an overt interpretation of what 2012 might be but instead created a modern vision of the classic portrait poster—one that incorporates the optimism of the Olympic Games with a bold iconic image of an Asian-American swimmer. The radiating lines, energetic color palette, and posterized dot screens provide a modern take on the psychedelic posters of the 1960s that dominated the Haight-Ashbury music scene.

Design Within Reach (DWR) is a distributor of mid-century classic and contemporary furniture for the office and home. DWR realized that though their residential business was thriving, they needed to strengthen their appeal to the design professional. Morla Design proposed issuing a tabloid, *DWR Profile*, that addressed topical design and architecture issues while showcasing new product offerings. The DWR signature red is used throughout the publication to unify all branding efforts and ensure an understanding that this publication is connected to DWR stores and catalogs.

Williams-Sonoma called upon Morla Design to create all consumer touchpoints for its Hold Everything retail stores. The scope of work included the catalog, shopping bags, packaging, labeling, gift boxes, and gift wrap. The catalog redesign required an analysis of product density, photography, typography, and branding devices. The redesign is considerably lighter in appearance, with the covers featuring a predominantly white image—chosen in order to allow the product to be the star of the photo, to capture the inspirational aspects of these products by evoking organization, and lastly, to permit the logo to stand out.

Kibu.com is an online company targeted to girls ages thirteen to eighteen. As with most dot-com start ups, Kibu was creating its branding on an ad hoc basis. Morla Design was retained to identify brand objectives, develop naming, create the identity, and design every consumer and trade touchpoint. This included product development, retail environments, newsstand magazines, broadband extensions, consumer advertising, and designing a hip Web environment that streamlined page count.

The palette is stylisticly trendy spotlighting hot colors. High-key orange was chosen as the basis for the dot identity so it would appeal to its young, fashion-conscious audience.

Ogilvy & Mather/
Brand Integration Group
New York/Los Angeles, USA

The Brand Integration Group (BIG) is Ogilvy & Mather Worldwide's design and brand experience division. Executive creative director Brian Collins runs the group as nothing less than a laboratory for imagination and storytelling. With a collaborative staff of artists, designers, strategists, filmmakers, playwrights, architects, cultural anthropologists, and writers, BIG works with some of the world's most prominent global brands. Design historian and writer Steven Heller, in *Print* magazine, called BIG "the leading incubator of design talent in advertising... Collins refuses to sanction timeworn notions, and indeed BIG's output never seems less than original."

BIG has offices in both New York and Los Angeles. Its work spans multiple disciplines, often in collaboration with Ogilvy & Mather colleagues and other creative agencies, to provide strong thinking and insights that affect the international cultural landscape. In *Fast Company* magazine, Collins summarized BIG's point of view by saying, "Brands are moving from a marketing model that says, 'I'm going to talk to you, and you better listen up' to an experiential model. Marketers need to focus on the way a brand gets brought to life tangibly, where it lives." It is these experiences that convey the brand, and BIG's design often creates them. "Design works to create meaningful attention that derives business. Design is connected to business results," states Collins.

BIG is an expert at reaching youth culture around the world. The designers understand how to speak to marketing-savvy young people who demand to be spoken to authentically. Collins explains, "Discerning youth can always smell phoniness. They are heavily marketed to, and have been from birth. They hate poseurs." This respect for the youthful audience shines through in all of BIG's work.

BIG's brief was to return to the original brand and revitalize Sprite's credibility with youth audiences. The designers were charged with creating branding, a packaging system, ambient marketing, and an advertising campaign that worked on a global basis. BIG found that the Sprite bottle was instantly recognizable because of its shape, dimples, and color, so it decided to leverage this in the work. The redesigned cans and bottle labels are shown above.

BIG found out what was authentic about the product. "We wanted our work to behave like Sprite," says executive creative director Brian Collins. BIG wanted to take the "Obey Your Thirst" campaign to a new level. Sprite was the first mainstream brand to embrace the hip-hop music and lifestyle and wanted to maintain this sensibility. BIG created a visual system that is customizable for specific markets. The top portions of the ads and posters (above and top right) change to incorporate graphics and typography specific to particular audiences, while the bottom halves remain constant and feature the Sprite bottle.

BIG also developed ambient marketing materials, such as subway posters (above), that allow Sprite to have a presence in daily urban life. These patterns of "chill camouflage" subtly show young people relaxing in a variety of ways. Viewers understand the message is about Sprite, mostly due to the color scheme and a sense of effervescence, but the message is less overt—there is no big Sprite logo in the camouflage. This type of design recontextualizes both the product and the idea of advertising itself.

"People don't see colors for what
they actually are; people see what
they bring to the idea of color."
—Brian Collins

BIG works to find out what is true about clients,
getting to the essence of the brand and then
interpreting these truths visually. "Rather than
find out what kids like and design the branding
around this, we find out what is true, and always
has been true, then find a way to express this
in a contemporary design that doesn't pander to
anybody," explains Collins. "Our work is about
authenticity. A true celebration of the product."

This philosophy also applies to the use of color.
BIG often returns to its clients' original brand colors.
The designers use colors that are linked to their clients, whether or not they are trendy or fashionable,
because they are instantly recognizable worldwide.
It is part of telling people what is true. Color supports
messages that must be distinctive enough to hold
interest and energy in a variety of places and media,
whether in a magazine, a bodega window, a product
held in the palm of the hand, or blown up ten stories
high on a billboard in Times Square. "The stories that
we have to live with every day, they're confusing,
so brands have an opportunity to get to clarity,"
Collins told *Fast Company.* "In my mind, branding
is about telling an understandable story, a unique
story, a memorable story. Tell your own true story."
Color is one of the ways BIG tells brand stories.

TIMES SQUARE CENTENNIAL

BIG renamed the Times Square Business Improvement District to become
the much more representative and empowering Times Square Alliance.
This group of business and community leaders works to revitalize and maintain
the Times Square area of New York City. BIG took its inspiration from Times
Square itself for the new identity system, which features neonlike typography
and hot neon pink as its signature color. Pink was chosen for its vibrancy
and visibility and because it is a little strange, just like that part of the city.

Coca-Cola is another global megabrand that BIG worked with to return to its essential truths and core appeal. The designers developed a campaign to reclaim "The Real Things'" realness. Eschewing the hyper-airbrushed otherworldly perfection of slick illustrations typically employed by soft drinks, executive creative director Brian Collins charged his staff with drawing and painting the products by hand. Imperfections, and the enriched depth of Coke's signature red color, expressed the brand in a more authentic manner and referenced the Coca-Cola Company's painterly visual legacy.

AT&T's new portable communication device, Ogo, was named by BIG to represent movement: "You can Ogo anywhere." Ogo is an entirely new word, yet it seems familiar and works in any language. BIG is sensitive to cultural associations with words, images, and colors, as so much of its work is implemented globally.

BIG created the identity and visual language for Ogo as well. "The streaming color spectrum graphic is an analog, a visual metaphor, for liquid lifestyle," explains Collins. "Kids don't want to be tied down or bound by limits. They'll be talking on their cell phones, searching the Web, doing their homework, watching television, and texting emails, all simultaneously! They are hypermultitaskers, and the world is being designed for them."

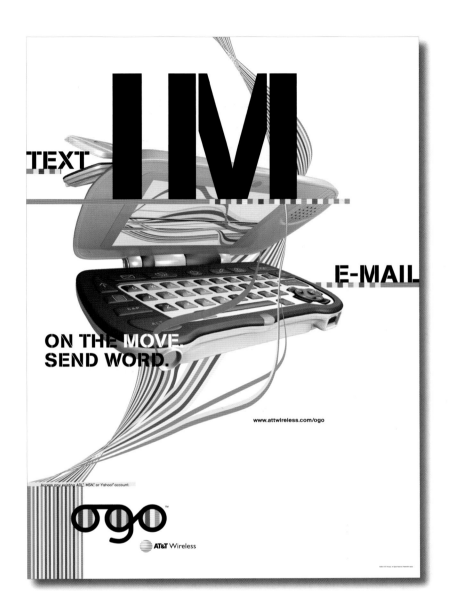

This series of ads, which also worked as bus shelter posters and print communications, prominently features the stripes of spectrum colors that become a flowing pattern. The colors play a role in signifying diversity of use as well as the diversity of Ogo's customers. BIG felt it was also important to show the Ogo product, a hand-held text messaging and email device, to demonstrate that Ogo is both an accessible product and brand—an inexpensive alternative to high-end products with the same capabilities. The black and white product photo contrasts with the streaming rainbow graphics. Bold typography, in black or knocked out to white, also works against the color patterns to provide a clear message.

Pentagram Design, Ltd.
London, UK

Pentagram is one of the world's premiere design companies. The firm is notable for its work, its unique business structure, and its longevity. Not given to the styles and trends of the day, Pentagram's work stands the test of time, and the company has been thriving for thirty-three years.

Pentagram is a multinational, multidisciplinary collaboration of designers who do print and screen graphics, product and environmental design, and architecture. The firm is organized around its nineteen partners, all practicing designers, who work with small dedicated teams and share minimal corporate infrastructure and support personnel. Pentagram has offices in London, New York, San Francisco, Berlin, and Austin. The 138 staff members are augmented by a worldwide network of collaborators who contribute to the capabilities of the firm. "I suppose it is a bit of a cult," mused partner John McConnell in an article in FT.com (a division of London's *Financial Times*). "I suppose that's how we behave in some ways."

Since its 1972 London founding, Pentagram, named for its original five principals, has been one of the most influential graphic, product, and architectural firms in the world. The firm is known for its many partners' unique talents and idiosyncrasies. In addition, the firm has always allowed for and encouraged many voices in design, rather than adhere to strict orthodoxies about the way Pentagram work should look. Pentagram has an ideology of idea-based design. This approach, says Randall Rothenberg in Pentagram Book Five, "asserted that design communicated both viscerally and intellectually, that it gratified the soul at the same time it satisfied the mind. As such, communication through design could not be achieved by the imposition of a strict set of rules or by the intrusion of an artistic vision." Each problem is unique and therefore invites a single solution appropriate to the problem—and that is essentially the designers' color philosophy as well. Color choices are made intelligently in keeping with the demands of each project.

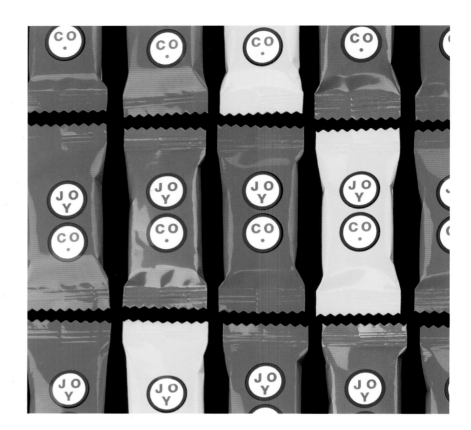

Pentagram was commissioned to create the new name and brand identity for the Spanish confectioner company GC Group (General de Confitería), which has manufacturing and sales offices throughout the world. The name and design are suitable for global use, with a name pronounceable in any language, and a palette of bright primary colors.

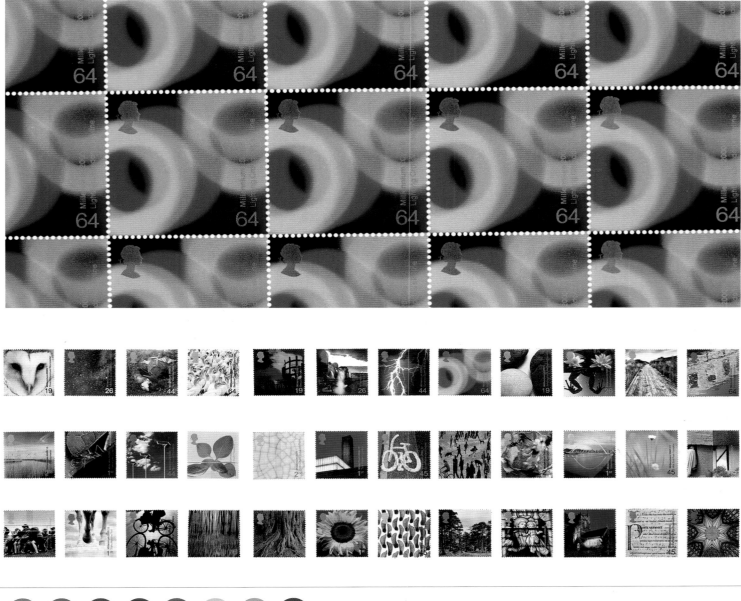

The Royal Mail invited Pentagram to design and art-direct a set of photographic stamps to celebrate the millennium. Various topics, including conservation, public spaces, and historic events, were chosen to celebrate and promote millennium-funded projects. The stamps were released monthly in themed sets of four; for example, "Above and Beyond" was released in January, and "Fire and Light" in February. Color plays an important role, speaking to variety and diversity, with each photographic image utilizing color in its own way. Taken as a group, the stamps offer a patchwork representation of the United Kingdom at the millennium.

Featured here are projects from Pentagram's European offices, representing the work of some of the eight partners and fifty employees, including principals David Hillman, John McConnell, Justus Oehler, and John Rushworth, along with designers Mathew Richardson, Jan Pluer, Liza Enebeis, Rob Duncan, and Hazel Macmillan. These pieces illustrate the variety of ways in which Pentagram's idea-based approach plays out in terms of color.

"Pentagram was set up by and for the design partners, so that they can continue their profession undisturbed, and can produce top-class design. Because good design satisfies the client, pleases the consumer, and also rewards the designer. We believe that good ideas, identity, function, aesthetics, and values make design unique."
—Justus Oehler, Partner, quoted in *Novum Magazine*

The Waterways Trust
Everyone valued, everyone involved
Review 2001/2002

The Waterways Trust is the only environment-focused trust for the conservation of waterways, including neglected canals, in mainland Britain and Northern Ireland. Pentagram designed the organization's identity and printed literature, which features black-and-white photography overlaid by a rich aquatic blue. The effect is rather somber, but the blue seems to symbolize the possibility that the stark landscape can be brought back to life.

Over the last twenty years, Pentagram has worked extensively for U.K. publisher Faber & Faber. Recent redesigns employ vibrant colors and strong typography. For the reprint of a series of Banana Yoshimoto's fiction (above left), Pentagram designed a visual language that unifies the body of work while suggesting the individual qualities of each book. At above right, the Faber poetry series is also devoid of imagery, again using color to express the central mood and emotional content of each book. The covers of the poetry series each use a limited palette of three colors: one for the author's name, one for the title, and one for the background. Yoshimoto's covers feature strong, Japanese character–based typography, while the poetry covers utilize Perpetua, a distinctive classical font.

Dragonfly Teas is a collection of rare organic teas developed for the European specialty whole and health food marketplace. Pentagram created the identity and packaging system. Wistbray Limited introduced Rooibos teas to the United Kingdom with the Dragonfly Tea range. This South African tea is renowned for its health properties and is naturally caffeine-free. Its distinctive rich red color inspired the package design.

The packaging for the entire range of teas creates a strong impact on the retail shelf and differentiates the products from other organic offerings. Using clean, austere typography, color-coded to each variety of tea, as well as the photographic device of wrapping a singular clear image around the package, Dragonfly Teas have a powerful presence at point of sale because of the uncluttered design. With its spare use of color, the teas' packaging stands out from the busy colorful graphics used by many organic tea brands.

The Splendor of Iran provides unprecedented insight into the traditions and contemporary life of one of the world's most enduring civilizations. The first comprehensive study of Persian culture since the 1930s, it is the result of a unique five-year collaboration combining Iranian scholarship, insight, and photographic access with international design and publishing.

A clear electric blue wraps the bilingual slipcase and provides a unifying band on the spines of the three-volume set. Most of the books' color comes from the series of specially commissioned photographs depicting ancient traditions that still affect the life and customs of present-day Iran in almost every sphere of human activity, including the decorative arts, science and medicine, philosophy, and poetry. The incredible scope and beauty of the subject matter is presented in an elegant design.

Segura, Inc.
Chicago, USA

Segura, Inc., is a multifaceted design and communications firm that specializes in print, collateral, branding, and new-media communications. The firm is one of five completely separate but united ventures founded by creative director Carlos Segura; the others are Segura Interactive The Web Division; 5inch, a product-based company that offers predesigned blanck CD-Rs; Thickface, an independent record label; and [T-26], a digital type foundry focused on the creation, distribution, and sale of original typefaces.

Born in Cuba and a refugee from the Cuban Revolution, Segura immigrated to Miami in the 1960s. He started as a musician who developed flyers for his band and later evolved into a self-taught designer/art director for ad agencies before moving to Chicago. There he founded Segura, Inc., in 1991. He and his partner/wife, Sun, head an international group of designers who produce graphic design, print advertising, logos, catalogs, annual reports, corporate identities, posters, and new media for carefully chosen clients. Segura says, "Whatever the medium, we create marketing messages people notice and respond to, with a distinctive sense of style and simplicity that stands the test of time."

Segura, Inc., deliberately stays small in order to be selective about the projects it takes on. The staff size is around ten people, including the two principals. This allows the designers to work on specific projects as well as control their destiny. "Everyone here is open-minded. It is essential. They all like what they do, and you can tell," notes Segura. The small size of the company also allows Segura to put his personal touch on each project. There is a high level of commitment to achieve top quality in all of the firms' work.

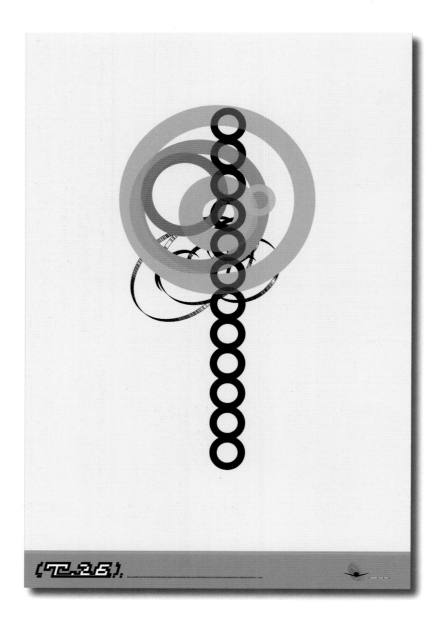

Segura's [T-26] digital type foundry was founded in 1994 in the middle of the postmodern typographic experimentation era. The company has become one of the best-known and globally influential modern type design foundries. [T-26] has stayed current, evolving from the grunge and hip-hop fonts that made it an instant hit with a new generation of computer-literate designers.

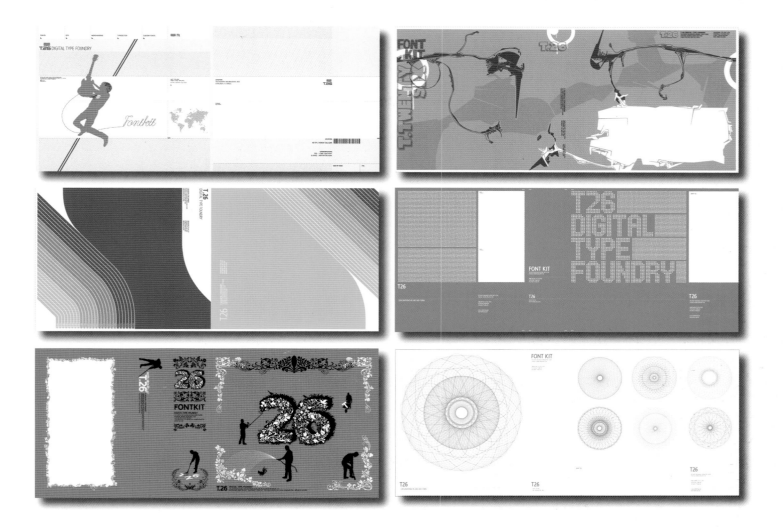

Segura, Inc., continually does interesting and innovative work on behalf of its subsidiary, [T-26]. Because the [T-26] fonts tend to break the traditional boundaries and notions of letterforms, so do its promotions. The poster (opposite) shows what might be called a classical approach with a modern edge, utilizing a subtle, nearly neutral color palette. The variety of [T-26] packs (above) are a riot of graphic styles and color schemes.

The [T-26] range includes more than 600 typefaces designed by 250-plus type designers from around the world. The packs therefore must convey the breadth of the product offering as well as provide demonstrations of effective font use. Segura sees the [T-26] packages as more "gift" than "sales pitch," so the pieces tend to resemble limited-edition artworks. The [T-26] kits are produced using a variety of techniques including letterpress, silkscreen, offset, and woodblock prints. (See also pages 216–217.)

T-26 DIGITAL TYPE FOUNDRY
1110 NORTH MILWAUKEE AVENUE, FIRST FLOOR
CHICAGO, ILLINOIS 60622.4017 USA. 1.888.T26.FONT (US.TOLL.F
TELEPHONE 773. 862. 1201. FACSIMILE 773. 862. 1214
E-MAIL INFO@T26.COM. WEB WWW.T26.COM

T-26 DIGITAL TYPE FOUNDRY
1110 NORTH MILWAUKEE AVENUE, FIRST FLOOR
CHICAGO, ILLINOIS 60622.4017 USA. 1.888.T26.FONT (US.TOLL.FREE)
TELEPHONE 773. 862. 1201. FACSIMILE 773. 862. 1214
E-MAIL INFO@T26.COM. WEB WWW.T26.COM

In an interview for a Taiwanese magazine, writer Jimmy Cuen asked Carlos Segura what was special about his studio. Segura replied, "We are very conscious of the client. We always deliver executions based on a relevant concept and not an out-of-context style . . . . We put the 'strategical' needs of a client ahead of our stylistic needs or desires, and we always target the intended market, even at the expense of the client's personal wishes." This approach of putting client needs first means that the firm has no set color philosophy. Color is chosen based on "whatever color we feel is appropriate for the task. We do not follow a rule for this, since it greatly depends on the body language of the project," explains Segura.

However, Segura does admit to the desire to blend and explore the fine art side of the business of design, not just the commercial. This edge remains visible in all of the studios' work.

> ## "Communication that doesn't take a chance doesn't stand a chance."
> **—Carlos Segura**

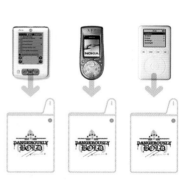

Express Jeans asked Segura to design a completely new kind of hang tag for its Dangerously Bold product line. The solution was hang tags that become usable as objects—for example, a cell phone or credit card case—once they are removed from the pants. The designs employ a variety of colors and type treatments meant to appeal to youthful audiences. Each hang tag was produced with a limited number of colors, but the hues chosen provide maximum impact when set against the denim of jeans.

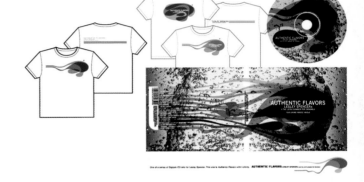

Segura, Inc., created the visual identity and music CD packaging for Lesley Spencer and the Latin Chamber Pop Ensemble's release called *Authentic Flavors.* The designers were charged with creating a design that represented the variety of the music. Their solution was to create a graphic of multiple colors joining into one element—a metaphor for the artists.

Steinbranding
Buenos Aires, Argentina

Steinbranding consists of more than sixty professionals and fifty designers committed to inspiring and revitalizing brands. Clients are primarily entertainment companies based in Latin America, but Steinbranding does have a variety of corporate clients and has branded two airports, one in Argentina and one in Armenia. Steinbranding calls their work "design for the southern hemisphere."

Primarily known for branding television networks and developing on-air promotions and show packages, the firm also creates off-air graphics in both print and Web formats. With more than fifteen years of experience in branding Hispanic television markets, Steinbranding has often handled the Latin American presence of U.S. television networks. Creative director Guillermo Stein says, "An unprecedented visual language characterizes our present and immediate future. The language is 'glocal'—where the global and the local blend. It is where all cultures connect without losing their identity." The firm strives to meet the unique challenges that the blending of cultures demands. Stein continues, " 'Glocal' design revolutionized the local market by connecting it to the world while keeping global languages from becoming empty and predictable."

Steinbranding is culturally sensitive and seeks to respect the differences that make each Spanish-speaking country distinct not only from one another but from the United States. The designers look to strike a new balance between cultures because, as they observe, "*Hispanic* is not the same as *Latino*. The challenge is how to capture these differences."

A large part of Steinbranding's work is to create the off-air promotions that coordinate with and support their on-air network ID packages. This is a poster for Colombia's Canal (á) television network. The lively graphics and bright colors are meant to appeal to Spanish-speaking audiences. Overlapping color blocks and rough typography give the poster a hand-hewn authenticity.

Creative director Guillermo Stein notes, "We do not impose a style; we search for the right style for each situation. Which is the most desirable visual language? The one that's able to bring out the potential of what each brand wants to communicate." For Cosmopolitan Televisión, a Spanish-language television network based on the Latin American version of the famous women's magazine, the visual language is about expressing modern femininity.

In the ID that also functions as a Web throw (advertisement of the website) (above left), Steinbranding used a dynamic hot pink graphic that moves through space, combining and recombining to form a voluptuous disk of color. The promotional poster (above right) plays with a different set of iconography representing contemporary women. A palette of muted primary colors provides a backdrop to a dressmaker's dummy that casts a shadow of a female form, creating depth and dimension while working as both a metaphor and a decorative device.

"Our task is not about undoing or changing a brand's essence. It involves, rather, shining a new light on it."

—Guillermo Stein

For El Gourmet, Steinbranding created programming and daily on-air promos, end pages and spots, as well as off-air graphics such as invitations, posters, and a website. The network and its companion online presence focus on food, celebrating its role in daily life and society. Steinbranding developed a cheerful, colorful, spontaneous design system with a sense of humor. In this network ID, El Gourmet on-air talent is featured in clean white uniforms against stark white backgrounds. Simple type and repeating patterns of food and beverage elements play behind the figures. The lime-green El Gourmet logo appears frequently to provide cohesive branding.

A slightly retro graphic style coupled with a muted palette work together to represent the alchemy and seduction of food—its scents, flavors, and colors. There is a Pop Art quality to this promotional poster's design that honors the pleasures of food as the symbolic center of a certain lifestyle. The art of good living is positioned as a great virtue to a sophisticated audience.

In this promo for El Gourmet's *Asador Urbano* (roughly translated, *Urban Grillmaster*), Steinbranding features the show's host together with graphic elements in the lime green of the network's identity. Lime green is used throughout all on-air and off-air graphics for El Gourmet as a unifying device. This particular green is fresh and lively and works well as a symbol for life and fine gourmet dining.

Steinbranding's work for the Hallmark Channel involved the adaptation of an international brand for Latin America. These projects are examples of what Steinbranding calls "glocal," the blending of the global with the local to form a brand message and graphic presentation that honors the best of both elements. The promo for the film *Estación Central* and for the "Romances" programming block features different color palettes, one subtle and one bold. Each color palette identifies a specific television show while supporting Hallmark's brand as a showcase for entertainment that is appealing to Hispanic audiences.

The Europa Europa Television Network's tagline is "Return to The Old World: Revalorization of Authentic Cinema." Steinbranding used this point of view as inspiration for this handmade, attention-grabbing orange poster (above), which promotes the channel in a fresh way. The graphics for *La Saga de Antoine Doinel,* a series that appears on the network, feature reds and blacks coupled with romantic script typography (lower right). Both designs work for an audience that is intelligent and modern.

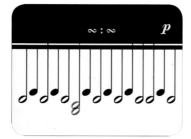

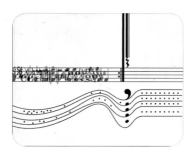

Film & Arts Network is a channel that seeks to reposition film as an art form. The challenge is to communicate and represent film as an artistic language and active movement rather than focus on the commercial aspects of movies. The graphics for the show *Big Bangs* (above) are stark black and white and take form as musical notations that mutate, multiply, move away, and then reappear.

The poster created to promote the network (above right) features the abstract play of transparent surfaces and typographic elements. A subdued palette of primary colors and grays subtly enhances the transparency effect of the floating planes of information. Both projects are sophisticated modern design solutions.

Gallery: Identity

1

2 | **K** (dot matrix letter K)

3 | for the dogs

4 | (R / G logo)

5 | THE MOHAWK TRAIL

6 | **SHOWTIME**

7 | selecti**on**

8 | (sun triangle logo)

9 | PARCO NAZIONALE DEL VESUVIO

10 | Let's *JetSet*

11 | **ATRIUM** *restavracija à la carte*

12 | (circle swirl logo)

13 | M I 2 0 06 SALZ ART 2006 MOZART SALZBURG

14 | (heart logo)

15 | (star logo)

16 | **FISH PACK** ®

17 | **Milk**

18 | **M** (sunglasses logo)

19 | POLNA SKLEDA *restavracija*

20 | **abc** family

21 | **LIVE** living in modern environments

22 | **redley**

23 | (rainbow A logo)

24 | (flag M logo)

25 | (castle pixel logo)

Gallery: Beverage

Hornall Anderson
Design Works

Powell

Hornall Anderson
Design Works

Hornall Anderson
Design Works

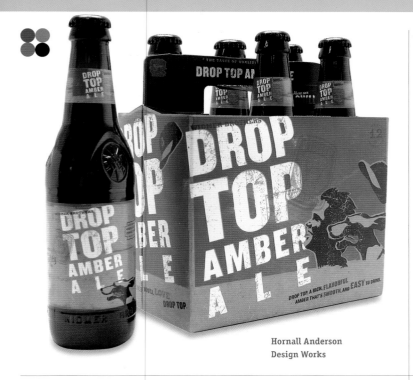

Hornall Anderson
Design Works

Chase Design Group

Carter Wong Tomlin

Hornall Anderson
Design Works

Gallery: Web

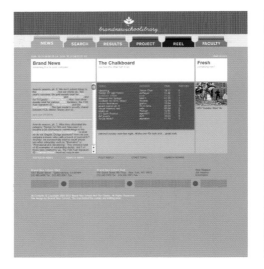

Brand New School

Michelle Moore Design

Hello Design

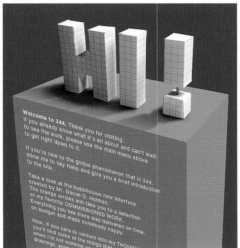

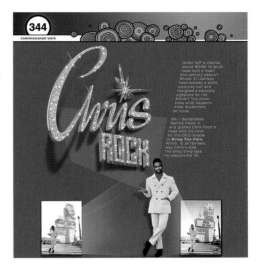

344 Design

Liska+Associates

Atelier Works

Gallery: Corporate Communication

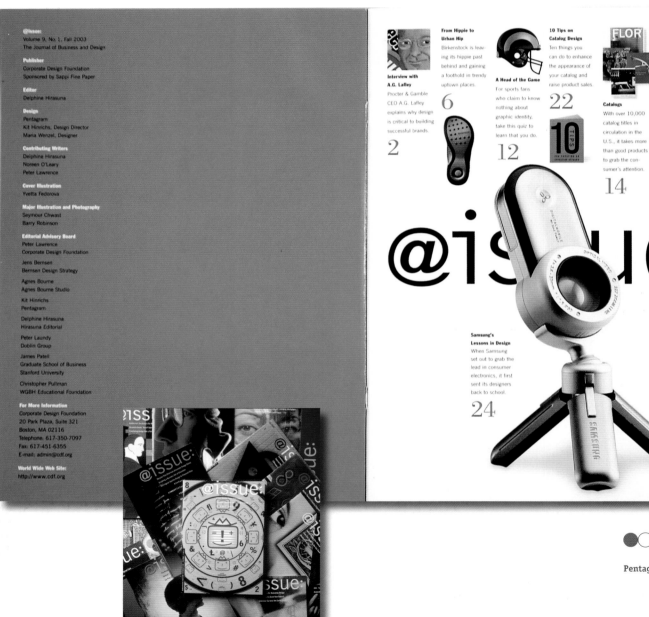

@issue:
Volume 9, No. 1, Fall 2003
The Journal of Business and Design

Publisher
Corporate Design Foundation
Sponsored by Sappi Fine Paper

Editor
Delphine Hirasuna

Design
Pentagram
Kit Hinrichs, Design Director
Maria Wenzel, Designer

Contributing Writers
Delphine Hirasuna
Noreen O'Leary
Peter Lawrence

Cover Illustration
Yvetta Fedorova

Major Illustration and Photography
Seymour Chwast
Barry Robinson

Editorial Advisory Board
Peter Lawrence
Corporate Design Foundation

Jens Bernsen
Bernsen Design Strategy

Agnes Bourne
Agnes Bourne Studio

Kit Hinrichs
Pentagram

Delphine Hirasuna
Hirasuna Editorial

Peter Laundy
Doblin Group

James Patell
Graduate School of Business
Stanford University

Christopher Pullman
WGBH Educational Foundation

For More Information
Corporate Design Foundation
20 Park Plaza, Suite 321
Boston, MA 02116
Telephone: 617-350-7097
Fax: 617-451-6355
E-mail: admin@cdf.org

World Wide Web Site:
http://www.cdf.org

Interview with A.G. Lafley
Procter & Gamble CEO A.G. Lafley explains why design is critical to building successful brands.

2

From Hippie to Urban Hip
Birkenstock is leaving its hippie past behind and gaining a foothold in trendy uptown places.

6

A Head of the Game
For sports fans who claim to know nothing about graphic identity, take this quiz to learn that you do.

12

10 Tips on Catalog Design
Ten things you can do to enhance the appearance of your catalog and raise product sales.

22

Catalogs
With over 10,000 catalog titles in circulation in the U.S., it takes more than good products to grab the consumer's attention.

14

Business and Design Classic
Clean, spare and elegant, the Eames molded plywood chair for Herman Miller established the look for the late 20th century.

32

Samsung's Lessons in Design
When Samsung set out to grab the lead in consumer electronics, it first sent its designers back to school.

24

Pentagram

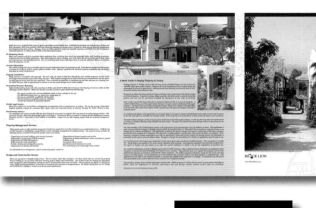

TENNIS VICTORIA ANNUAL REPORT 2004

Chimera Design

CE75

KROG

Usine Des Boutons

Gallery: Poster

Collaboration
A lecture
Thursday, February 8th
at 10:00 am
Portfolio Center
125 Bennett Street
Atlanta, Georgia
404.351.5055

Chermey Steff & Geissbuhler

Dinner with Steff Geissbuhler
An AIGA Member only event

Come dine with Steff Geissbuhler
at Bluepointe Restaurant in Buckhead on
Wednesday, February 7 at 6:00 p.m.
Please R.S.V.P. to Peter Borowski, AIGA President at
770.395.3960 or pborowsk@clari.com.
This event is limited to the first 10 AIGA members
who RSVP by Monday, January 29.
Each guest is responsible for the cost of
their own meal and beverage.

Chermeyeff & Geismar

Marci Boudreau

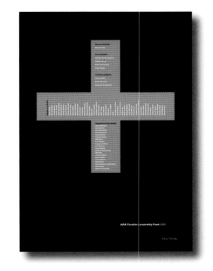

AdamsMorioka

Ogilvy & Mather / Brand Integration Group

Segura, Inc.

blue river design

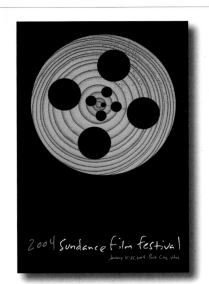

AdamsMorioka

Glossary

Achromatic is the state of possessing no discernible hue and being without color.

Additive colors are produced by superimposing red, green, and blue light rays. All of these colors combine to create white light. Computer monitors and television screens use additive color.

Advancing colors appear nearer to the observer than receding colors. Warmer, higher-chroma, and lighter-valued colors tend to advance.

Afterimages are complementary color images generated by the eye in response to overstimulation or retinal fatigue.

Analogous colors are hues that are adjacent on the color wheel.

Blends are areas of an image that transition from one color to another. Blends are also called *graduated tints* or *graduations*.

Brilliance is the quality of high light reflection and strong hue typically found in saturated colors.

Brightness is the amount of light reflected by a particular color. Brightness is also called *value*.

Chroma is the relative purity or strength of a hue, or its freedom from white, black, and gray. Chroma is a synonym for *intensity* and *saturation*.

CIE stands for Commission International de l'Eclairage, an international color consortium.

CMYK stands for cyan, magenta, yellow, and black, the colors of the subtractive color system used in offset lithography printing. They are also called *process colors*.

Color is a perceptual sensation created in the human mind in response to certain wavelengths of electromagnetic energy that constitute the visible spectrum of light. Human perception of and response to these wavelengths is affected by many factors including physiology, psychology, language, and culture.

Colorimetry is the technical term for the scientific measurement of color.

Color constancy is the ability of the human eye and brain to perceive colors accurately under a variety of lighting conditions, compensating automatically for any differences.

Color correction is the process of adjusting the color values of an image to correct or compensate for errors in photography, scanning, or separation.

Color reduction is the process of reducing the number of colors in a digital image in order to make the file smaller.

Color schemes are harmonious color combinations that use any two or more colors. The six classic color schemes are *monochromatic, analogous, complementary, split complementary, triadic,* and *tetradic* (also called *double complementary*).

Color separation is the process of separating images and artwork into cyan, magenta, yellow, and black in preparation for printing.

Color space is the range of colors achievable by any single reproduction device.

Color tetrads are sets of four colors, equally spaced on the color wheel, that contain a primary color, its complement, and a complementary pair of intermediaries. The term can also indicate any organization of color on the wheel forming a rectangle that could include a double split complement.

Color triads are sets of three colors, equally spaced on the color wheel, that form an equilateral triangle.

Color wheels are circular diagrams representing the spectrum of visible colors and illustrating their relationships.

Complementary colors are two colors opposite each other on the color wheel. They tend to intensify each other when used together and create a neutral color when mixed.

Cool colors are greens, blues, and violets.

Duotones are two-color halftones reproduced from a black-and-white or color photograph. The term can also mean a halftone image rendered in two colors.

Fugitives are ink colors that easily fade or deteriorate.

Gamut is the range of colors available within a certain color space.

Ground is the area that surrounds the central element or figure in a composition. Another term is *background*.

Harmony is a pleasing subjective state that occurs when two or more colors are used in combination.

Hue is the attribute of a color, defined by its dominant wavelength and position in the visible spectrum, that distinguishes it from other colors. The term can also indicate the name of a color.

Intensity is a synonym for *chroma,* which is the relative purity or strength of a hue.

Intermediate colors, also called *tertiary colors,* are made by mixing a secondary and a primary color together.

Lightness is the blackness or whiteness of a color.

Luminance is the brightness of a color.

Metamerism is the undesirable phenomenon that occurs when two colors that appear to match under one set of light conditions do not match under another set of conditions.

Monochromatic is the state of containing only one color.

Neutral colors are black, gray, white, browns, beiges, and tans. They do not appear on color wheels.

Optical color mixing, also called *partitive color,* is a perception of color that results from the combining of adjacent color by the eye and brain.

Palette is a group of colors used by a designer in a specific design.

PANTONE Matching System (PMS) is a patented system of inks, color specifications, and color guides used for reproducing colors.

Primary colors are pure hues from which all other colors can be mixed. They cannot be made by combining other hues. The artist's mixing primaries are red, yellow, blue (RYB); the additive primaries are red, green, blue (RGB); and the subtractive primaries are cyan, magenta, yellow (CMY).

Process color is four-color reproduction that uses four printing plates, one for each of the subtractive primary colors: cyan (process blue), magenta (process red), yellow (process yellow), plus black (process black).

Profile is the colorimetric description of the behavior of an input or output device that can be used by a computer application to ensure accurate transfer of color data. A profile describing the color space used during the image creation or editing should ideally be embedded in the image so it can later serve as a reference for other users, software applications, or display and output devices.

RGB stands for red, green, and blue, the primary colors of the additive color model.

RYB stands for red, yellow, and blue, the artist's primary colors, which are the basis of much color theory taught in art and design schools.

Saturation is the measure of the purity of a hue as determined by the amount of gray it contains. The higher the gray level is, the lower the saturation. Saturation is a synonym of *chroma.*

Secondary colors are made by mixing two primary colors.

Shades are hues mixed with black to form another darker color.

Simultaneous contrast is a human perception anomaly in which colors are affected by adjacent colors.

Spot color is a single solid or screened color printed using one printing plate, as opposed to a process color printed using two or more plates.

Subtractive colors are those produced by reflected light. Cyan, magenta, and yellow inks printed on white paper absorb, or subtract, the red, green, and blue portions of the spectrum. Subtractive color mixing is the basis of printed color.

Tertiary colors are formed by combining two secondary colors or by combining a primary with an adjacent.

Tints are hues mixed with white to form another lighter color. The term also refers to a solid color screened to less that 100 percent to create a lighter shade.

Tones are created by mixing a pure hue with its complement or gray.

Triadic schemes are color schemes using three colors that are spaced evenly around the color wheel.

Value is the relative lightness or darkness of a color. High value is light; low value is dark.

Vanishing boundaries occur when two different solid color areas of exactly the same value are placed next to each other; the hard edge separating the two colors seems to soften or disappear.

Vibrating boundaries occur when two different solid color areas, usually near complements of near equal value, are placed next to each other; the result is a noticeable optical fluttering effect.

Visible spectrum is the full range of visible hues. The rainbow is a naturally occurring manifestation of the visible spectrum.

Warm colors are reds, oranges, and yellows.

Directory of Contributors

88 Phases
8444 Wilshire Boulevard, 5th Fl.
Beverly Hills, CA 90211
USA
323.655.6944
www.88phases.com

344 Design
Los Angeles, CA
USA
626.796.5148
www.344design.com

Addison Company
20 Exchange Place
New York, NY 10005
USA
212.229.5000
www.addison.com

Atelier Works
The Old Piano Factory
5 Charlton Kings Road
London NW5 2SB
UK
44.020.7284.2215
www.atelierworks.co.uk

BASE Design
Rue de la Clé 5
1000 Brussels
Belgium
32.2.219.0082
www.basedesign.com

blue river design
The Foundry, Forth Banks
Newcastle-upon-Tyne NE1 3PA
UK
44.0191.261.0000
www.blueriver.co.uk

Marci Boudreau
Los Angeles, CA
USA
323.377.3504

Brand New School
2415 Michigan Avenue, Bldg. H
Santa Monica, CA 90404
USA
310.460.0060
www.brandnewschool.com

Robert Bynder
Los Angeles, CA
USA
323.459.5996
www.bynder.com

C375
Tarik Zafer Tunaya Sokak 3/6
Gumussuyu
Istanbul 80040
Turkey
90.212.249.77.09
www.C375.com

Cahan & Associates
171 Second Street, 5th Floor
San Francisco, CA 94105
USA
415.621.0915
www.cahanassociates.com

Carbone Smolan Agency
22 West 19th Street, 10th Floor
New York, NY 10011
212.807.0011
www.carbonesmolan.com

Carter Wong Tomlin
29 Brook Mews North
London W2 3BW
UK
44.020.7569. 0000
www.carterwongtomlin.com

Andreja Celigoj / Art: Tečaji
Hruśevo 95
1356 Do Brova, Slovenia
386.516.760
www.art-tecaji.com

Chase Design Group
2255 Bancroft Avenue
Los Angeles, CA 90039
USA
323.668.1055
www.chasedesigngroup.com

C&G Partners
116 East 16th Street
New York, NY 10003
USA
212.532.4460
www.cgpartnersllc.com

Chimera Design
102 Chapel Street
St. Kilda, Victoria 3182
Australia
61.39593.6844
www.chimera.com.au

**Concrete Design
Communications, Inc.**
2 Silver Avenue, Main Floor
Toronto, Ontario M5K 1K2
Canada
416.534.9960
www.concrete.ca

Crosby Associates
203 North Wabash Avenue #200
Chicago, IL 60601
USA
312.346.2900
www.crosbyassociates.com

Durfee Regn Sandhaus
Los Angeles, CA
USA
www.drsstudio.com

Dynamo
5 Upper Ormond Quay
Dublin 7
Ireland
353.1.8729244
www.dynamo.ie

Fauxpas Grafik
Hardturmstrasse 261
Zurich, CH 8005
Switzerland
00411563 8638
www.fauxpas.ch

Format Design
Grosse Brunnen Strasse 63a
Hamburg
Germany
49.040.32086910
www.format-hh.com

Gee + Chung Design
38 Bryant Street, Suite 100
San Francisco, CA 94105
USA
415.543.1192
www.geechungdesign.com

Getty Publications
1200 Getty Center Drive
Los Angeles, CA 90049
USA
310.440.7300
www.getty.edu

**Green Dragon Office
(Lorraine Wild)**
948 South Muirfield Road
Los Angeles, CA 90019
USA
www.greendragonoffice.com

Hello Design
8684 Washington Avenue
Culver City, CA 90232
USA
310.839.4885
www.hellodesign.com

**Hornall Anderson
Design Works, Inc.**
1008 Western Avenue, Suite 600
Seattle, WA 98104
USA
206.467.5800
www.hadw.com

Hunter Gatherer
191 Chrystie Street #3F
New York, NY 10002
USA
212.979.1292
www.huntergatherer.net

Johnson banks
Crescent Works, Crescent Lane
Clapham, London SW4 9RW
UK
44.0.20.7587.6400
www.johnsonbanks.co.uk

Karlssonwiliker, Inc.
536 Sixth Avenue
New York, NY 10011
USA
212.929.8064
www.karlssonwiliker.com

KBDA
2558 Overland Avenue
Los Angeles, CA 90064
USA
310.287.2400
www.kbda.com

Kinetic
2 Leng Kee Road
Thye Hong Centre
#04-03A Singapore 159086
65.63795320
www.kinetic.com.sg

Kontrapunkt
Knezova 30
1000 Ljubljana
Slovenia
386.15756606
www.kontrapunkt.dk

KROG
Krakouski Nasip 22
1000 Ljubljana
Slovenia
386.41.780.880
www.krog.si

Victoria Lam
Los Angeles, CA
USA
www.particularbear.com

Lippa Pearce Design
358a Richmond Road
Twickenham, TWI 2DU
UK
44.0.208744 2100
www.lippapearce.com

Liska & Associates
515 N. State Street, 23rd Floor
Chicago, IL 60610
USA
312.664.4400
www.liska.com

Lorenc + Yoo Design
109 Vickery Street
Atlanta, GA 30075
USA
770.645.2828
www.lorencyoodesign.com

Uwe Loesch
Brugger Muhle
Mettmanneer Strasse 25
40699 Erkrath
Germany
49.211.55.84.8
www.uweloesch.de

Louey/Rubino Design Group, Inc.
2525 Main Street, Suite 204
Santa Monica, CA 90405
USA
310.396.7724
www.loueyrubino.com

LUST
Dunne Bierkade 17
2512 BC The Hague
The Netherlands
31.0.70.363.5776
www.lust.nl

Marco Morisini
Via Boncio, U9
61100 Pesaro
Italy
328.4781280
www.marcomorisini.com

Michele Moore Design
Los Angeles, CA
USA
323.528.7404
www.mooregraphicdesign.com

Methodologie, Inc.
808 Howell Street #600
Seattle, WA 98101
USA
206.623.1044
www.methodologie.com

Mevis & Van Deusen
Gelderseude 101
1011 EM Amsterdam
The Netherlands
31.20.6236093
mevd@xs4all.nl

Morla Design
463 Bryant Street
San Francisco, CA 94107
USA
415.543.6548
www.morladesign.com

Motion Theory
321 Hampton Drive #101
Venice, CA 90291
USA
321.396.9433
www.motiontheory.com

New York Times Magazine
229 West 43rd Street
New York, NY 10036
USA
212.556.5920
www.nytimes.com

Ogilvy & Mather/
Brand Integration Group
309 West 49th Street
New York, NY 10019
USA
917.797.5291
www.ogilvy.com

Pentagram
11 Needham Road
London W11 2RP
UK
44.0.20.7229.3477
www.pentagram.com

Pentagram
204 Fifth Avenue
New York, NY 10010
USA
212.683.7000
www.pentagram.com

Pentagram
387 Tehama Street
San Francisco, CA 94103
USA
415.896.0499
www.pentagram.com

Ph.D
1524a Cloverfield Boulevard
Santa Monica, CA 90404
USA
310.829.0900
www.phdla.com

Powell LLC.
10 West 18th Street, 8th Floor
New York, NY 10011
USA
212.260.6604
www.powellny.com

R + MAG Graphic Design
Via del Pescatore 3
80083 Castellammare di Stabia
Italy
00.39.081.870.5053
www.remag.it

Sagmeister, Inc.
222 West 14th Street, Suite 15A
New York, NY 10011
USA
212.647.1789
www.sagmeister.com

Samata Mason
101 South First Street
Dundee, IL 60118
USA
847.428.8600
www.samatamason.com

Segura, Inc.
1110 North Milwaukee Avenue
Chicago, IL 60622-4017
USA
773.862.5667
www.segura-inc.com

Steinbranding
El Salvador 5675
(C141BQE) Buenos Aires
Argentina
54.11.4776.4422
www.steinbranding.com

Stone Yamashita Partners
355 Bryant Street #408
San Francisco, CA 94107
USA
415.536.6604
www.stoneyamashita.com

Stripe (Jon Sueda & Gail Swanlund)
5015 Eagle Rock Blvd, Suite 212
Los Angeles, CA 90041
USA
323.255.1979
www.stripela.com

Sweden Graphics
Blekingegatan 46
SE-116 64 Stockholm
Sweden
46.0.8.6520066
www.swedengraphics.com

Andrea Tinnes
Das Deck
Schliemannstrasse 6
10437 Berlin
Germany
49.0.30.44.031.629
www.typekut.com

Usine De Boutons
Via Guido Franco, 99B (PD)
35010 Cadoneghe Padova
Italy
39.049.8870953
www.usine.it

Vrontikis Design Office
2707 Westwood Boulevard
Los Angeles, CA 90064
USA
310.446.5446
www.35k.com

Walker Art Center
1750 Hennepin
Minneapolis, MN 55403
USA
612.375.7600
www.walkerart.org

Winterhouse Editions
P.O. Box 159
Falls Village, CT 06031
USA
860.824.5040
www.JHWD.com

Michael Worthington
Los Angeles, CA
USA
michael@counterspace.net
www.counterspace.net

Thank you.

Bibliography

Albers, Josef. *Interaction of Color.* New Haven, CT: Yale University Press, 1963.

Carter, Rob. *Digital Color and Type.* Mies, Switzerland: RotoVision, 2002.

Fraser, Tom, and Adam Banks. *Designer's Color Manual: The Complete Guide to Theory and Application.* San Francisco: Chronicle, 2004.

Hollis, Richard. *Concise History of Graphic Design.* London: Thames & Hudson, 2001.

Itten, Johanes. *Itten: The Elements of Color.* New York: Van Nostrand Reinhold, 1970.

Kobayashi, Shigendbu. *Colorist: A Practical Handbook for Personal and Professional Use.* Tokyo: Kodansha, 1998.

Meggs, Philip B. *Type & Image: The Language of Graphic Design.* New York: Van Nostrand Reinhold, 1992.

Ocvirk, Otto G., Robert E. Stinson, Philip K. Wigg, Robert O. Bone, and David Cayton. *Art Fundamentals: Theory and Practice, 8th Edition.* New York: McGraw-Hill, 1998.

Poynor, Rick. *Obey the Giant.* London: August Media, 2001.

Sutherland, Rick, and Barb Karg. *Graphic Design Color Handbook: Choosing and Using Color from Concept to Final Output.* Gloucester, MA: Rockport, 2003.

Sutton, Tina, and Bride M. Whelan. *The Complete Color Harmony.* Gloucester, MA: Rockport, 2004.

Walch, Margaret, and Augustine Hope. *Living Colors: The Definitive Guide to Color Palettes Through the Ages.* San Francisco: Chronicle, 1995.

Wong, Wucius. *Principles of Color Design: Designing with Electronic Color.* New York: Van Nostrand Reinhold, 1997.

Web Resources

Additional useful color information can be obtained from the following websites.

www.about.com
www.adobe.com
www.albersfoundation.org
www.bartleby.com
www.color.org
www.colormarketing.org
www.colormatters.com
www.findarticles.com
www.pantone.com
www.wikipedia.org
www.wordiq.com

About AdamsMorioka

Based in Beverly Hills, AdamsMorioka's philosophy of clarity, purity, and resonance has served as a catalyst in the design community since 1994.

Sean Adams and Noreen Morioka have been globally recognized by every major competition and publication including; *Communication Arts*, AIGA, *Graphis*, The Type Directors Club, The British Art Director's Club, *ID*, and the New York Art Director's Club. In 2000, The San Francisco Museum of Modern Art exhibited AdamsMorioka in a solo retrospective. Adams and Morioka hold the honor of being named to the ID40, citing them as two of the 40 most important people shaping design internationally.

AdamsMorioka's book, *Logo Design Workbook* was released in April 2004. AdamsMorioka's clients include ABC, Adobe, Gap, Old Navy, Frank Gehry Associates, Nickelodeon, USC, Sundance, and The Walt Disney Company.

www.adamsmorioka.com